Diamonds in the Dirt

STORIES FROM A JUNKYARD GIRL

LAURIE RIEDMAN

Copyright 2024 by Laurie Riedman
Text © Laurie Riedman
Photographs © Laurie Riedman
Design by van der Sterre Design

First Edition 2024
Published by Badass Sisterhood Press USA

ISBN: 979-8-9901393-2-9

Content clarification: This book contains references to childhood sexual abuse.

This book is a labor of love
and is dedicated to "little Laurie."
You are brave, strong, and resilient.
I am so grateful you are a storyteller.

Author's Note

This is my truth. This story is about sharing my childhood—unique and filled with happiness and trauma. I have tried to connect the dots, some painfully clear and others frustratingly fuzzy, of my memory.

Memory is a curious and confusing thing. When recalling childhood trauma and emotional overwhelm, memories can be like listening to music from a scratched record: They skip and jump.

The stories I share in *Diamonds in the Dirt: Stories From a Junkyard Girl* weave a powerful narrative of growing up among discarded car parts and an interesting and somewhat crazy cast of characters in a rural Connecticut junkyard. There, I survived childhood abuse by harnessing the creative power of pretend to spark life-saving resiliency, turning my childhood circumstances into adult gifts. As I more deeply explored the difficult and painful times, I unexpectedly unearthed more joy, laughter, and love than I had ever imagined.

The collection is arranged by theme rather than chronologically, allowing me to bridge those gaps and more clearly share the arc of where I've been and where I am. Many stories jump in time within the story because that is how I could tie the gaps together and see the themes emerge. Readers, please be aware that some of the stories contain references to childhood sexual abuse.

Thank you for being here.
Laurie Riedman

Contents

INTRODUCTION

The Power of Dirt

WE WERE SURROUNDED BY IT.

We lived in it.

I often felt like I was a piece of it. I believed I would never be rid of it.

The entrance to the junkyard led to a steep hill. During the descent, a circle of cliffs rose, formed bit by bit as Dad sold the ombre red and gold dirt as gravel fill for nearby construction projects. It was a steady source of income for us. The junkyard got lower as the cliffs and Dad's bank account got higher.

Cars would enter and exit, kicking up a whirling cloud of dust that landed wherever it wished. Thin films of dirt became a part of us—on us, on our toys, in our mouths, and under our fingernails. Dirt was a constant companion.

As a kid, it was heaven.

Rain puddles became mud baths. We made elaborate recipes in hubcaps. The metal saucers perfectly shaped our brown culinary delights. Heads bent in concentration, we'd work on perfecting the ratio of water to dirt, knowing the result would be a beautiful masterpiece inverted onto a decorative cardboard platter.

Some days, we were in the Wild West. We'd dig and use our plastic sifter from the beach pail set to pan for gold. We would always find something of interest in the basin: a rock with specs of "real gold" as well as other treasures like copper pennies partially patinaed or encrusted with verdigris among coins of greater value, odd bits of metal, broken glass, or rubber shards.

Eventually, Mom would summon us, give us the once-over, sigh (often with a smile), and direct us to get in the bathtub. We would march forward, knowing playtime would continue when we were submersed in bath water.

Mr. Bubbles or a can of Crazy Foam at the ready—we'd squirt each other clean. The fun, soapy foam sprayed out of the can like Dad's shaving cream and would become beards, mustaches, and crowns. We'd write with it on the bathtub walls and build floating foam towers. The challenge was how high to make the tower before it slowly lowered into the water like an iceberg melting into the sea.

Barbies float naked, hair matted from too many baths or bad haircuts. Mom let us use her stackable orange Tupperware measuring cups to rinse our hair and have water fights. I remember a set of plastic squirt guns—assorted colors and sizes! The plugs long lost, they were now used for bath-time target practice—usually on my little sister and brother. Yes, until we three were too big—or too old—we bathed together, taking turns to stand up to make room for one of us to "swim."

Once out, wrinkled and wrapped in towels, our clean, naked bodies partially reflecting in the steamy big bathroom mirror, my little sister and I would wipe a circle of steam away so we'd have a little window to watch ourselves. We'd dance, pretending to be the Lawrence Welk backup singers. We were lean and elegant in shiny long dresses, our towel turban–wrapped heads became our fancy updos.

By that point, the only evidence of our day of outdoor play was a dirty brown ring around the tub.

We were clean—but to others—we could never be.

We were a different kind of dirty. A dirty that can't easily be washed off.

It took me years—make that decades—to get the "dirt" off.

It wasn't just from my improper relationship with Mr. P as I satisfied his perverted desires but also a multilayered silent shame that others bestowed upon us.

I have a memory of playing in one of our mud puddles. I was probably five or so—happy, immersed in experiential and creative play—when out of the corner of my eye, I saw two men standing and staring at me and my little sister with contorted faces. We were squatting down around the brown puddle, and they towered above us. I heard one of them say something like, "Look at the junkyard kids. Poor things. Living here in squalor. Look how dirty they are. Such a shame."

They were customers who came for a cheap used auto part and noticed us playing, probably scantily clad and muddy as heck. I remember the look in their eyes. I didn't know what it meant then, but I felt it. A sting deep inside—a pain—told me something was wrong, that I was wrong.

What those customers didn't know was that another man's junk can be a treasure. You just have to dig for it.

Some of the messages I internalized came from kids at school. Playground banter from bullies rang in my ear as they made fun of where I lived, as well as the making fun of the thick glasses I had to wear.

"Hey, Junkyard Girl!"

"She's just like one of her junkyard dogs—nasty and smelly."

"Four Eyes! Four Eyes!"

"She's just a piece of junk!"

"She lives in a dirt pit—she belongs there."

On the outside, it appeared as if this didn't faze me. Distancing myself became one of the superpowers I developed, especially as Mr. P got me to do things I knew weren't right. I never let it look like it bothered me.

The truth was I was being eaten from the inside out—only I didn't know it.

I heard and somehow believed it, although part of me knew the truth. A part of me—a resilience—grew as I fought to survive. My truth hidden by layer upon layer of those messages. My authentic self shellacked by a shell of unspoken shame others piled on me.

By becoming who you expected me to be, I survived. I was good at it, too.

Despite the junkyard dirt packed in the soles of my sneakers and forever under my fingernails, I became a high school honors club member, student body officer, and cheerleading captain. I sang in the chorus and played major parts in all the high school dramas and musicals.

I became the collegiate coxswain who led her novice crew to an undefeated season, the college freshman who got the lead in the play, and the girl to "lose" her "real" virginity to an early college love who eventually broke her heart.

It was messy being me. Finding me. That dirt had lodged in my soul.

Yet I did it. Unearthing the real me from under that hard armor I built up from the shit others threw my way.

It would be years later, after college, marriage, and kids, that I'd do the work to uncover the truth. Instead of operating as being less than everyone else, being terrified you'd "find out" who I really was—a fraud, a fake to be pitied or judged—I'd mine the real me. Slowly, I began to excavate and recognize who I was underneath all that shit, underneath all that dirt. Steadily digging deep, I realized I wasn't being seen for who I really was. I was not some piece of junk—some junkyard dog.

It was as if, so many years later, I looked straight into those mud puddles and saw a clear reflection.

The ability to be so fully immersed in whatever story I needed saved me. My childlike wonder evolved into adult-like curiosity.

Four Eyes had new eyes.

I could see that growing up in the junkyard and experiencing sexual abuse as a child—certainly while fraught with challenges, difficulty, and pain—also held magic and strength and birthed my spunkiness. What hurt me saved me.

I uncovered and explored the dirt—the hurt—and healed it. I am fully alive and allow myself to feel passion and desire in my marriage. I am grateful I somehow found the right partner to be alongside me as I worked to reignite the parts of me that had been hidden for decades.

I see the miracle that my family—all of us—having experienced the struggles and joys of growing up in a junkyard, have become the people we are today, learning to accept and love one another more deeply as the years march on.

I recognize where the holes have been inside me for most of my life. Today, I know it's possible to fill them. And fill them I do.

After years of support from my husband, family, and countless types of therapy, weekend retreats, reading books, and doing the work, I could shout it out with pride: "YES, I AM THE JUNKYARD GIRL!"

I had been an uncut diamond among discarded car parts and broken glass. My broken bits—the sharp shards of glass shattered from childhood trauma, the other challenges that came my way, the lies I believed about myself, the personas I took to make my way safely in the world—were necessary. I wouldn't want it any other way. They made me who I am today. Each pain, each sharp edge, was slowly worn down like sea glass or a diamond, becoming smoother with each wave.

I am a sixty-three-old diamond, shining for all to see.

PROLOGUE

———

Innocence

MY BODY IS HEAVY WITH EXHAUSTION AS I LEAN AGAINST THE DOORWAY OF MY infant daughter's room. Peering inside, I notice the nightlight casting a delicate swath of mini-moon and -star shadows on the pink carpet, forming a magical path of twinkling light leading to her crib.

I allow myself a moment of idleness and feel how beat my body and mind are. I gaze at the room, my heart swelling with pride as if I were an artist looking at a painting I'd just created.

I can make out her small peanut bundle shape, expertly swaddled in the white, pink, and blue flannel receiving blanket just as the nurse in the hospital instructed me to do. Although she is safe in the nursery across the hall from our bedroom, I worry that I moved her into the crib too soon. It looks so large, out of scale, with her tiny body. A sigh I didn't know was there escapes. The desire to scoop her up and put her back in the bassinet next to our bed comes over me, but I know my husband, Rich, will calm me with the logic that we need our rest, and she'll be just fine. I worry: Will I be too tired to hear her when she cries?

I sigh again. My heart is full. The wonder of her creation still astounds me. All those months of preparation. Making sure I was eating right and remembering to ingest those horse-pill-sized prenatal vitamins. Getting things organized at my business and hiring a senior employee I trust to keep my clients happy while I take minimal maternity leave. The trip to Europe to introduce my new employee to my largest European clients—with Rich, who wouldn't let me go without him—and the official note from my doctor assuring the airline I wasn't about to give birth on the plane. All those hours picking out the nursery furniture, pink and white striped wallpaper, a white-eyelet baby comforter with matching bumpers that I'm currently looking at. All waiting for her to arrive.

I recalled all of it—especially the evenings: Rich and I sitting side by side, me propped up by a growing pile of pillows to get comfortable, as I poured over *What to Expect When You Are Expecting*. Boring Rich with facts and figures of her growth each week. I confess to having read sections repeatedly—especially about going into labor—as if I were studying for a test.

I had worried about both my babies' growth and development—the one I had birthed just five years earlier that I named Riedman Communications and the one I had been carrying like I had swallowed a basketball.

I'd spent so much time putting things in place to assure my clients and myself that things wouldn't change. That I'd still be available. That my dedication to the business and their public relations needs would not suffer. That I'd still be me.

All that races through my mind in milliseconds as I stand here, dirty onesies and spit-up cloths in hand. *Liz is here. I'm a mom. I did it.*

Perhaps it's hormones, but I am awash in an overwhelming maternal unconditional love that must have grown within me just as she did. My heart fills with a cocktail of love, fear, and hope as my milk percolates in my still-sore breasts. I stretch my back, but my eyes stay glued to her tiny body. I listen to her breath, my own matching her cadence. I watch her little chest move up and down, and her limbs occasionally involuntarily twitch. My mind ticks. My sweet daughter. My firstborn. My. . .my. . . .

She looks so tiny in the large crib. I am struck by the realization of her vulnerability and my responsibility.

Then I feel it. A tiny spark of tightness in my chest. I'm holding my breath, and my muscles are tensing.

What is it I am feeling? It feels familiar.

It grips me tighter.

Is it fear?

My mind races to the heaviness of this obligation Rich and I have. We are parents. My open motherly heart restricts. Liz is my first baby. She is my responsibility. I will care, love, and protect. She was born almost two weeks early, and I question my readiness.

Oh, my god.

I was once Liz. I was just as vulnerable. My parents couldn't protect me from Mr. P. What makes me think I can protect her?

The enormity of this task hits me.

I crumble to the floor. I hear quiet sobs, and it isn't until I feel a touch on my arm and hear Rich's soothing voice and warm arms around me that I realize those sobs are coming from me.

That's the moment it started. My lifelong journey to understand and reconcile my childhood, to dig deep to understand and confront what I gained and what I lost. What was my fault, and what wasn't? What happened, and what didn't? I didn't know this then, but this was when I began to turn away from who I was pretending to be toward being who I am today.

What follows are personal essays from me, the junkyard girl. Stories of how I found love, loss, joy, and lifesaving resilience despite an unconventional childhood surrounded by a crazy cast of characters, discarded car parts, shards of glass, and love.

PART ONE

Life as a Junkyard Girl

Junkyard Girl

THE SCHOOL BUS MOANED UP THE HILL, GRINDING ITS GEARS. IT CAME TO A SCREECHING halt just at the tippy-top of Killingworth Road hill—often called Watson Hill. The bus doors swung open and released us—the Watson kids—at the start of our long, dusty driveway. My younger sister Maddy and I kicked up sparkly specs of sand with scuffed Buster Browns as we meandered down the dirt driveway. We didn't talk. In our own worlds, we blindly followed the drive as it snaked down the hill to our small cedar-shingled home perched smack dab in the middle of my dad's junkyard.

Instead of a white picket fence, shrubbery, and lawn, my home was surrounded by twin peaks of used tires, black rubber mountains, and piles of mismatched hubcaps waiting for some poor soul to pick through to find the mate to the one lost on some roadway. A babbling brook wove behind the house and all along one side of the junkyard, looking as if it didn't quite belong there.

If that weren't enough, the junkyard—and our home—was also situated square in the middle of a gravel pit. Thanks to a giant bulldozer and new home developments nearby that needed "clean fill," the gravel pit surrounding the junkyard became broader and deeper as Dad sold the dirt to make up for lost revenue as junkyard sales became leaner and leaner. The gravel pit surrounding us provided a much-needed additional source of income as Dad mined the dirt underneath us.

Hundreds of cars and trucks in various stages of undress—missing hoods, doors, windshields, engines, transmissions, and much more—dotted the ten acres of wooded and barren land.

Beside our humble home, on a wide patch of red and brown dirt, sat the customary metal swing set—missing a few parts like everything else around us—yet still sporting two swings with faded red metal seats that, in the summer sun, were too hot to sit on. The slide was a bit treacherous as it was seriously bent and missing one of the supports at the bottom. The swing set appeared rather suddenly one day. I'm pretty sure it was due to a hasty junkyard barter resulting in some poor kids waking up to their swing set missing but their dad's car finally working.

Of course, we also had a tire swing. We did, after all, have no shortage of tires.

At the age of eight or nine, I had no idea how odd it was to live in a junkyard. To me, living there was normal and magical. To all five of us kids, it was home.

For me, my little sister Maddy, and baby brother Jack, the junkyard was the only home we knew. My older brother and sister—Ryan and Cindy—had lived in Queens when they were born to our mom and a different dad. I didn't discover they were my stepsister and stepbrother until my early teens. They were my big sister and brother, but because they were older than me—Ryan is nine years older, Cindy is six, while Jack, Maddy, and I are two years apart—I don't remember having many adventures with Cindy and Ryan. They were busy being teenagers when I was a child. For the most part, Maddy and Jack were my partners in crime among the junk cars, creek beds, and sand pits.

Growing up in a junkyard created quite a range of life experiences—some good, many dangerous and dysfunctional—that ignited my self-reliance and love of story, any story. Ahhh, the deliciousness—and safety—of getting lost in the woods behind our house or deep in the junkyard for so many hours we'd emerge as if we were drunk, dazed by the power of pretend. Mom's booming voice yelling for us from the house would eventually drag us back to reality, hungry and tired but happy.

It wasn't just our imaginations that took us places. We had the bus.

Magic Bus

YOU COULDN'T SEE IT FROM THE HOUSE, BUT IT WAS THERE, ITS DENTED NOSE pointed uphill, and its back two rusted wheel rims were going nowhere, buried in the ground. Tufts of grass grew from the dirt where the tires should have been. To adults, that faded yellow, rusted-out school bus was grounded. But to us, it flew like the wind.

Our bus was missing a few windows and more than three-quarters of the bench seats, but the door handle still worked. You know the one. The black plastic lever to the right of the steering wheel that opened the door still worked. With a deliberate but simple push and tug, those long, cracked, and dirty vertical glass doors magically opened and shut on command—allowing us to get on and off at any destination we chose.

On most school days, after making our way down the dusty drive to the house, we'd dump our school stuff—vinyl lunchboxes and beat-up book bags overflowing with worksheets, forgotten permission slips, and homework. My sister Maddy and I would whip up a pitcher of Kool-Aid and grab whatever cellophane-wrapped Hostess treat my older brother Ryan may have left in its flimsy cardboard box. And before you knew it, we were off to the junkyard, pigtails flying, sneakers skidding, and kicking up dust past piles of hubcaps and rusted wheel rims. Up the hill, we would go to where our afternoon adventure awaited.

The moment we were on the bus, and those doors safely closed behind us, my sister and I and—if we were feeling generous our little brother Jack—were ready for the ride of a lifetime.

Despite living close to the Long Island shoreline in Connecticut, we got to the beach on the ocean only a few times. But that didn't stop the bus. A premier destination, we'd plan for the beach, coordinating the trip a few days prior via cryptic phone calls to the neighbor kids we sometimes played with and drawing detailed maps and itineraries. On the appointed day, we'd all arrive at our "bus stop" with our swimsuits and flip-flops on, sand pails in hand, and toys at the ready for any possible sandcastle construction job that might come our way.

We'd create elaborate stories featuring exciting characters. Sometimes, we became rich, sophisticated women with thick, Parisian accents like those straight out of the *Eloise in Paris* book I had taken out of the library. Or we'd be exotic hula dancers in grass skirts like we'd seen Marcia and Jan Brady wear when they traveled to Hawaii on *The Brady Bunch*.

Our characters lived extraordinary lives and had adventures and special powers like the characters of *The Swiss Family Robinson*, *Mary Poppins*, *Bewitched*, or *The Jetsons*. Sometimes the characters were "well off," from families with parents who had endless supplies of quarters for arcade games or lived in mansions by the sea, or had fairy godmothers or servants to grant their every wish.

Invariably, during one of our bus trips, one of us would be designated "the mom" or "the driver." They controlled the situation—often being very strict at our beach destination. They cautioned us not to go in the water right after eating for fear of drowning or would quickly put someone in "time out" under our make-believe umbrella just because they could.

Thanks to the open space behind the missing bench seats at the back of the bus, where the emergency exit door used to be, we'd have the perfect opening to jump off the bus only to line back up at our bus stop as another character in our ongoing saga. This way, the driver would have an endless supply of people to pick up on our journey, and the four of us could become a steady stream of interesting characters waiting to board.

Of course, we'd fight over who could be the driver. I admit I took that seat a bit more often than others. I liked to be in charge.

As soon as we got on the bus as one character, we'd run to the rear, grab a new prop—a hat or perhaps mom's old nightgown (which became an elegant slinky dress)—jump out, and scoot back around to the front to wait in line again at the bus stop. As soon as the door swung open and the driver waved to us, we'd hop back on as new passengers.

Imagination was our navigation system on the bus, and creativity was our fuel. We traveled to galaxies, met Martians, and befriended aliens; we solved mysteries with Nancy Drew and the Bobbsey Twins. Once we were inspired by a new game called Operation I had played at a friend's house. We were doctors saving lives by performing emergency surgeries—just in time.

The bus gave us a destination, a story, and a much-needed break from the reality of living on the wrong side of town.

Nicotine and Love

THE SMELL OF LOVE IS BITTER NICOTINE LACED WITH SWEET WHITE SHOULDERS perfume. Whenever I smell that combination of opposites, I think of my mom.

Born and raised in Brooklyn, Mom was tough, intelligent, and gorgeous. Her name, Glory, described her perfectly.

She was a force to be reckoned with. She married young, and after having two children, Glory caught her husband in bed with his secretary.

It was the late 1950s, a time when it was customary to ignore a wandering husband and stay in the marriage and the safety it provided—especially with two young kids. But Mom was a badass and left.

She landed in Connecticut to live with her parents temporarily. They had moved from the city to the quaint suburbs of Connecticut when Grandpa sold his Brooklyn beauty shop to open a small shop in Middletown.

It wasn't long before Mom met my handsome Dad in his army uniform at a USO dance. Less than a year later, they were Mr. and Mrs. Watson, living in a trailer in a junkyard in the tiny town of Higganum.

I know Mom loved Dad, but she also was a realist. I'm not sure if she confessed to this to me or I some how figured this out, but I imagine after moving in with her parents after her divorce, she couldn't burden them by living there forever. She was most certainly hurt but also practical. As a result, she may have felt insecure at the prospect of raising her two young children, Cindy and Ryan, on her own. Mom was no romantic. She accepted things for what they were and moved on.

Mom never spoke about her first husband, and in fact, I didn't even know Ryan and Cindy were my stepbrother and -sister and that my dad wasn't their "real" dad until I was in my teens. Sadly, their father wasn't in the picture for most of their lives.

I could tell by my mom's mother Grandma Josephine's demeanor whenever she came over to our house (it was as if she was afraid to touch anything for fear of catching something) that she didn't think Mom could be happily married to Dad, living smack dab in the middle of a junkyard. What Grandma didn't get was that happiness had nothing to do with it.

Instead of the quiet suburban life—including the lovely home surrounded by a white picket fence, appropriate shrubbery, and lawn my grandparents imagined for their daughter—Mom was living in a trailer surrounded by, well, junk.

Dad, while no prize catch, was funny, entertaining, and intelligent. Perhaps Mom felt like she and her family would be okay with Dad. And, for the most part, she was right.

I can't imagine Mom loved where we lived. But she was a woman who dealt with the cards she was given.

She had a great smile and had many friends but could seem rough and distant to an outsider. We always knew she loved us. She worked hard to make life in the junkyard feel normal and acceptable. She sometimes wore a large button that said, "If you don't like my peaches, don't shake my tree." She didn't need the button to exude that attitude. When mom called, we came running—like when we were headed to a social at St. James Church.

"Lauuuuuurrrriiiieeeee! Maddyaaaaaa! Jaaaaaaack!" she yelled at the top of her lungs. At the same time, her eagle eyes scanned down the hill and into the junkyard to see if she could spot us among the hundreds of rusted-out cars in various forms of undress. "Where are youuuuuuu?"

It took a while for her words to reach us, but cigarette in hand, she rounded us up and into the car. She did not check that our hands and faces were washed before we left. Instead, with the vehicle in motion, her frantic glances in the rearview mirror confirmed we were not presentable.

There we were—Maddy, age eight; Jack, age six; and me, age ten—lined up in the back seat. We all sported reddish-brown clown smiles from the making—and pretend eating—of mud pies that moments before we had carefully crafted in molds made from upside-down hubcaps.

Mom just sighed and took a drag of her cigarette. She had the "once-over" plan.

When we reached our destination, we hopped out of the car, lined up, and waited. The inspection was coming, and we knew the drill.

First, Mom performed her own once-over, carefully applying red lipstick as she tipped the rearview mirror and puckered to ensure complete coverage of her plump lips. I don't recall a signature shade, although lipstick was one of her few luxuries—a drugstore treat. She didn't go anywhere without lipstick.

The cigarettes varied, too, though always a cheaper brand. Smooshing the butt in the car ashtray, she smoothed her hair, grabbed her purse, and exited the car. We were next.

She approached and crouched down, her face just inches from ours. I could feel the rhythm of her hot, nicotine-drenched breath on my cheeks. I knew what was coming.

Accessing and grabbing my face with one hand, she slipped her fingers of her free hand between her red lips to moisten them with brownish saliva. Using the wetness on her fingers, she vigorously rubbed dirt spots off my face. I tried to move my head away and back to avoid her washing, but the process repeated—lick, rub, lick, rub. When somewhat satisfied, she'd move on to Maddy or Jack.

I never felt clean, but I did feel loved.

I don't know when or how I understood Mom's love. I just felt it.

Mom's love came from a profoundly primal place. It wasn't the hearts and mushy love I imagined my friends had—no hugs for no reason. Mom's hugs were purposeful and practical—no cuddles on the couch.

Mom's love was an undercurrent lurking below the chaos. Her love was always there; it just came in fits and starts. It would appear at a moment's notice and then go into hiding. Mom's love was vital to my survival, but ultimately, she couldn't save me.

Like her distinctive aroma, her love was a combination of opposites—tough but tender. I remember how her love got me through my first seventh-grade dance.

I had burst into the house and was upstairs on my bed before my ride home left our dirt driveway. Mom heard my sobs from her bedroom below and came to the stairwell. "Laurie, what's wrong, honey? What happened?"

I crept out of my room and slumped at the edge of a worn step at the top of the stairway. Mom stood at the bottom in her nightdress, looking up at me from under her crazy bedhead hair.

Holding my head in my hands, I started to cry. She let out a heavy sigh. In an instant, she was sitting right next to me. The bittersweet scent of White Shoulders and nicotine meant Mom was near.

I waited, wanting her to hold me and tell me everything would be okay. That's what Carol Brady would have done for one of her bunch. When that didn't happen, I gathered the strength to tell her about the dance.

Wiping my eyes on the soft lavender sleeve of my new Danskin top, I said in a voice so low she had to lean in to hear, "Mom, no one asked me to dance. I felt so stupid just standing there while everyone was dancing." Hands covered my face; my shoulders hung heavy and shook with sobs.

Feeling her hot, familiar breath on my wet cheek, I knew her heart was as heavy as mine. I felt close to her as if she were hugging me tight.

She didn't reach out. I waited patiently, sitting by her side, feeling the space between us as if it had a life of its own.

Eventually, breaking the silence, I sniffled and continued my story.

"So I just left to go to the bathroom, where I stayed the rest of the night crying in the stall." A few sobs slipped out, and my voice found the strength to share the evening's most bitter betrayal.

"Mom, my friends never even noticed I was missing. When it ended, Robin found me in the bathroom and didn't even ask what was wrong! Couldn't Robin see I had been crying? She just kept going on and on about how much fun I missed and who she danced with. I thought she was my best friend."

Mom sighed, stiffening a bit, then said softly, "I'm sorry that happened, Laurie. It sounds awful. It hurts when our friends aren't there for us." She paused as if she were thinking of something else. "I'm so, so sorry. But you know what? I'm sure you'll feel better in the morning. Things always feel better for me in the daylight. It's late. Let's try to get some sleep. Off to bed now."

She headed downstairs to her bedroom. I went up to mine, tucked in by the lingering smell of her love, imparting warmth and hope and easing my pain. Mom may not have studied psychology, but she understood the power of being heard.

Glory Laurie

"LAURIE!" YELLED MY SISTER MADDY AFTER ANSWERING THE PHONE. "IT'S FOR YOU."
Grabbing the receiver, my teenage voice said, "Hello," while without skipping a beat, the voice on the other end replied, "Glory? Is this Glory? I want to talk to Glory, not Laurie." I relinquished the phone to Mom for the hundredth time.

I used to wonder why she gave me a name that sounded similar to hers. Was it because she wanted me to be like her?

I doubt it. Planning wasn't one of Mom's strong suits. Despite having nine months to pour over baby name books and pick a name for me, I've been told that hours after my birth, I was wrapped in a white, blue, and pink receiving blanket under a card that read: Baby Watson (It's a girl!). Soon after, the card on my bassinet in the hospital nursery sported the name Laurie, destined to be confused with Glory for most of my childhood.

Mom loved her soaps and got hooked on several of them during her pregnancy with me. The story goes that Mom caught an episode—not sure if it was *One Life to Live*, *As the World Turns*, or *Guiding Light*—where the storyline involved a character named Laurie. I am not sure what the character Laurie did, but whatever it was apparently impressed my mom.

Mom shouldered most of the responsibilities of raising us—ensuring we were properly clothed, putting food on the table, and paying bills. Dad was in the background. Despite this, Mom seemed to handle it without cracking. She was solid, sometimes shaken, but recovered quickly. She had to.

We'd often hear her mumbling to herself as she sat at the kitchen table, a lipstick-stained smoldering cigarette butt in the ashtray, sipping her ninth cup of Maxwell House coffee, looking somewhat defeated. Or was it depressed—or both?

Yet, hours later, she'd appear with freshly applied bright lipstick, her hair teased and in place, ready with her trademarked red-lined smile to take on whatever the day might deliver.

Mom was always stealthily on our side. Deep in the top drawer of her dresser, she collected a hidden stash of crumpled bills—mostly ones, fives, tens, and an occasional twenty she skimped from money Dad gave her for essentials. We used that "mad money" for a rare treat—a foot-long hotdog at Higgies, a popular roadside haunt in town, or an old-fashioned soda at the worn Woolworth's fountain counter in nearby Middletown. Sometimes, those crinkled bills would help purchase a big-ticket item, such as a layaway deposit on a new winter jacket and boots, or Christmas gifts for us at Bradlee's.

Mom wasn't detail-oriented, and I don't think she liked to drive. She was a city girl. Driving was a skill she learned later in life out of necessity. Despite getting lots of practice carting Maddy to gymnastics, me to guitar lessons, Jack to drum corps, or to St. James church for a council meeting, Mom was a fast but careless driver. New bumps or scratches gave the junkers she drove additional character.

Mom didn't like to drive. I didn't, either.

Perhaps an early indication that driving would not be my strong suit was the predicament I found myself in just hours after obtaining my driver's license at the age of sixteen.

I had been so excited to get my license. Mom kindly invented an errand for me to do—alone in the car—shortly after returning from the DMV with my brand-new "temporary" paper license. She desperately needed milk from the grocery in town. I was only too happy to pick some up.

Feeling a twinge of fear but primarily new-found freedom, I peeled out of our dirt driveway onto Route 81, kicking up a cloud of dirt as I accelerated a tad too much down the hill.

I resisted putting on the radio as I recall the driving instructor telling us not to have any distractions when we were new to the road.

Taking that first solo drive, I was comforted by the security the wooden blocks Dad had previously installed to both the gas and break pedals so I could reach them and see over the steering wheel. This was due to an obvious problem we discovered months earlier as I took the maroon Chevy Nova for a spin with my learner's permit in my pocket and my mom in the passenger seat: the driving challenges of a sixteen-year-old who was less than 4 feet 11 inches tall.

These were the days before ergonomic seat adjustments existed.

We discovered my driving challenge the first time I drove, months ago, after obtaining my learner's permit. As I attempted to accelerate and see over the steering wheel, the car made a fast-slow pattern, jerking its occupants back and forth. This was due to how I had to move—jostling my body up and down, alternating as I stretched my foot to make contact with the gas pedal but losing sight of where I was going. To rectify the issue, I quickly fell into a rhythm, slinking down in the seat to step rapidly on the gas and then jumping back up, straightening up to look up over the steering wheel to see where I was going.

Apparently, I could drive, but only in using this fast-slow combination of—stepping on the gas (acceleration), looking up to see (foot off the gas, slow down), and then repeating again and again as the car lurched forward slowly. After that experience, Mom instructed Dad to do something about it, and he installed wooden blocks on the pedals.

So back to that official virgin solo drive.

I don't quite know what happened, but I remember going safely under the speed limit, taking turns around Higganum Reservoir carefully—hands gripping the steering wheel at ten and two. Glancing in my rearview mirror, I noticed an impatient car coming up very close to my bumper.

I nervously watched the car inch up behind me, worried it was going to hit me. Suddenly, I felt a crash; my glasses flew off, and my car stopped. I reached for my glasses, and when I put them on, the image that came into focus was deep blue water looming in front of me. It was then I realized the car—engine still running—was teetering over a guardrail, which was the only thing preventing the car (with me in it) from sliding down a steep embankment into Higganum Reservoir.

I believe that was my first indication that daughter-like-mother—or Laurie-like-Glory—driving would not be my strong suit either.

Hungry for Home

AN ITALIAN SAYING COMES TO MIND WHEN I RECALL SPENDING TIME WITH MOM'S parents, Grandpa and Grandma Martinez: *"Chi si volta, e chi si gira, sempre a casa va finire,"* which translates to "no matter where you go or where you turn, you'll always end up at home."

A home can be so many things. Our home nestled in the junkyard was undoubtedly a lot of things, yet it was Grandma and Grandpa's home that gave me something I—and I think all of us—desperately needed.

They had built this home after leaving the bustle of Brooklyn to open a small hair salon in nearby Middletown, Connecticut. Eventually, they retired here. Their home felt like home to us all.

The house was just a fifteen-minute drive from the junkyard, but it felt like another world. Located just off a wooded road that zigzagged a bit, their home sat behind traditional New England stone walls and had an actual blacktop driveway leading to an attached garage. The house was a simple ranch surrounded by shrubs, flowers, and a lawn. Yup. A real lawn that had to be mowed.

We'd go almost every Sunday for supper.

Once we entered the front door, my body would relax into the warmth of whatever was cooking in the kitchen. Grandpa would see me, smile, and scoop my tiny frame up from the floor. He'd hug me tight with his thick, muscular arms and carry me into the kitchen, where he'd sit me up on the counter. From my perch atop the worn laminate countertop, I was his helper—an eager culinary apprentice, ready to assist.

Together we'd measure and pour the pale-yellow semolina flour directly from its paper sack into the big ceramic bowl resting beside me.

Grandpa would be wearing his white kitchen apron, speckled with red sauce stains ghosted by Grandma's unsuccessful bleaching efforts. The thin apron ties barely met after making the circumference of his jolly girth.

Italian opera playing from the HiFi in the adjacent living room, he would sing along as he added the egg, his fat fingers gingerly holding it with one hand and expertly cracking it along the side of the bowl. He'd smile and say, "Ahhhhh, a good one, huh? You watch an' learn, little one."

Years later, as I watched professional chefs on TV cooking shows, I'd remember that he cracked his eggs like they did—in a practiced, one-handed, quick motion.

A pinch or two of salt and a swirl of olive oil from a large tin can made green circles in the flour. His strong fingers gently guided mine as we punched and kneaded the dough.

Later, after the thick but not completely uniform shapes came out of the pasta maker, he'd hand the strings to me, and I'd place them over the tops of the cabinet doors to dry. We'd make a mess, but boy, was it fun.

Mom and us kids would make the trip most Sundays for an early supper. I don't remember Dad coming, but he must have been there or came occasionally. My sister Cindy told me that Grandma had no problem relinquishing the kitchen to Grandpa as she wasn't the best cook and knew it. Cindy only remembered that Grandpa didn't cook when his sisters visited because they could COOK!

Mom followed in Grandma's footsteps; she didn't like to cook either, and it showed. That must have been the reason my sister Cindy and I became pretty good cooks, as we'd take over cooking duties as soon as we could reach the knobs on the stove. Dad was famous for his over-cooked hamburgers, which he made late at night. We'd find the evidence in the morning. Cloudy congealed grease in a frying pan still on the stove and a dirty plate with smears of ketchup on the counter.

The real chef in the family was Grandpa Martinez. He made dishes from his homeland, Sicily, Italy, that oozed love, care, and family. As soon as we came through the front door, our noses were greeted with the familiar yet unique combination of the earthy and spicy smell of his cigar and the sweet acidic aroma of his "gravy"—tomato sauce that had been simmering for hours on the stove—we knew Grandpa was in the kitchen.

While I felt safe and loved there, there was an air of formality we were not accustomed to. Grandma kept an orderly home. The complete opposite of the chaos in ours, it was comforting.

Their bedroom was adjacent to the gleaming disinfected kitchen, featuring two twin beds neatly made with frilly crocheted pillows atop puffy floral quilts that had a sheen to them. They looked soft and comfy, but the fabric was stiff and slippery. When I sat on them, I'd slide off.

A gold-trimmed mirrored tray on her dresser held fancy glass perfume bottles in exotic shapes with pink rubber atomizers coming out at odd angles, calling to be touched and squeezed.

Even the clear plastic covers on the formal sofa and chairs in the living room felt welcoming, even though they made funny noises when you sat down. They stuck to our skin, no matter the season, requiring us to peel ourselves off when we wanted to get up. Just like the furniture, I was protected there.

Grandpa was fun, too. He liked to play games, and they had things there we didn't have at home. Next to "his" chair, there was a pipe holder that he'd let me spin, as well as a fancy cigar box we weren't allowed to open.

I remember a wooden rocking horse at their house that I liked to climb on and ride, although it did squeak a bit. I think it was originally for Ryan when he was a toddler, and each of us—in turn—rode it back and forth throughout the years.

I'd often sit on Grandpa's wide and comfy lap, and I'd shake a bit when he laughed. Often a nickel and a dime would appear from his shirt pocket, and he'd hold them out in his palm for me to choose.

"You can only have one," he'd say. I would quickly snag the nickel, thinking I was getting the better deal because it was thicker and bigger. The day I picked the dime, he smiled and gave me a squeeze, "Well done, smarty pants," he said. I don't think we ever played that game again.

In all weather, we'd be outside. We were so bundled up in snowsuits it was a miracle we didn't topple over. We'd make snowmen and angels in the snow and slide down their little driveway hill in proper plastic saucer sleds they kept in their garage.

Summertime was the best. We'd play croquet, setting up the misshaped metal hoops in irregular patterns. The game would inevitably end when one of us got mad, and the wooden mallets would become weapons. Sometimes Grandpa would let us play with his brightly colored bocce balls. We'd roll the heavy balls around the yard, making up our own rules.

They had a small stream running through the backyard. Grandpa built a little dam with stones, creating a makeshift waterfall and overflowing pond just large enough for us to wade in and get wet. It was our own natural pool. I loved the *plunk-thunk* sound substantially sized stones would make when they hit the water and sank after I tossed them. I loved how clear and cold the water was. My toes would become numb if I were in it too long, and I'd limp when I got out.

After dinner, the adults would gather on the enclosed porch for coffee and watch us kids as we'd chase and catch fireflies at dusk. Maddy and I ran around to corral them into thin, multicolored plastic cups. We'd try to get as many of them as possible in one cup—no small feat. Have you ever tried to keep fireflies in a cup while you attempted to add even more?

We aimed to have enough "light power" to make the cup appear like a colored light bulb. I don't remember if it ever worked how we imagined, but it was fun trying.

I remember hearing the murmur of the conversation between Grandma, Grandpa, and Mom on many of those nights. Grandma would sit next to Grandpa and look up at him, leaning on the table. She was what others called "petite" with a small, bony frame and a long nose that belonged on her proportionately long, wrinkled, freshly powdered face. Her chin jutted downward, yet she held her head high. Mom said Grandma was always "put together." Her tight lips were probably permanently stained red by how often she reapplied lipstick from the gold metal Estée Lauder tube she kept in her purse. Mom must have gotten her similar lipstick habit and shade from Grandma, except Mom only applied if we were going somewhere. Grandma wore her lipstick even when she was at home. I always wondered if she was simply being prepared for unexpected guests or if she wore it to bed at night.

I loved how she kept her precious lipstick tube at the ready in her purse. I loved her purses, especially the soft dark leather pouch trimmed with a shiny gold metal hinge that opened like a butterfly. When she firmly snapped it shut, a gold clasp announced itself with a loud final click.

Grandma grew up in Spain and wore colorful dresses with matching scarves and sensible but well-cared-for low-heeled pumps in a coordinated color. Even her everyday "house dresses" seemed fancy with their bright, alive floral patterns and contrasting colored zig-zagging piping outlining the patch pockets.

Grandma had golden hair set and curled weekly. She certainly knew how to do it herself, but sometimes she had it done at their salon and years later at a salon on Main Street in Middeltown. She kept her curls in place with those funny metal clips framing her face when she went to bed at night.

She wasn't as touchy-feely as Grandpa, but Grandma always had little treats for us. It might be a new jump rope still in the cellophane packaging or a brand-new shiny set of metal jacks with a red rubber ball that had all the bounce still in it. And she always had a bottle of bubbles on the porch. Maddy and I would blow bubbles from the steps and watch as they moved and floated in the wind. We loved it when our eyes could follow them until they touched and burst on rocks and the lawn below.

Grandma paid "good money" to have a ceramic bust made of her cat Winny, which stood like a sentry near the front door next to the fireplace. It was an orange tabby that had long since died. I think Grandma had the ceramic made to memorialize her feline family member. I always thought it was looking at me no matter where in the room I was. We would feed it pretend treats.

Years later, as adults, someone found the statue, and it became a game to move it around from house to house. Ryan may still have it.

One Sunday, we were there for dinner as usual. Ryan was mowing the lawn, and I was on the back porch with Grandpa. He was trying to fix something, and I was playing beside him. It was 1966, and Ryan was just about to enter high school. I was five years old, and Maddy was three.

The details are hazy, but I was sitting on his lap. Suddenly, he set me aside, slumping over. I must have thought he was taking a nap, so I quietly continued to play next to him; I'm not sure for how long. At some point, I've been told that I went into the house and said something like, "Shhhh, Grandpa is asleep." The next thing I remember, everyone was screaming and crying, and we were rushed to a neighbor's house.

Much later, Mom came to the door, collected us, and told us in the car that Grandpa had gone to heaven. He'd had a massive heart attack and died on the porch.

Cindy and Ryan started to cry. Mom did, too, but put the car in gear and backed out of the neighbor's driveway. I wasn't sure what was going on. Could he still come visit from heaven and play with me? Did Grandma go with him? I had just seen him. He was taking a nap. Didn't they try to wake him up? I had so many questions I didn't ask. I just sat there, looking out the window. I had Maddy's sleeping head in my lap. As muffled sobs surrounded me, sadness filled the car, eventually spilling over to me, and I cried.

The house felt different after that, now that Grandpa wasn't there. It smelled different, too.

Cinderella After the Fireman's Ball

I WOKE TO A WHIFF OF ALCOHOL AND NICOTINE FROM HIS WARM BREATH ON MY neck as he bent over to pull me out of bed. It took some effort to extract my little legs from the bedspread and sheets that were tangled and twisted around me. I was startled and afraid for a split second, but as soon as I realized who it was, a warm feeling crept from deep inside and slowly showed itself as a sheepish, sleepy grin on my tiny face.

I had hoped he'd come for me, like he had last time, in the heat of the moment, running up the stairs to my bedroom to scoop me up and out of my slumber.

I could hear the music getting louder as he carried me closer to the impromptu dance floor in the middle of our kitchen.

The familiar voice of Slim Whitman crooning "Beautiful Dreamer" came from the sophisticated reel-to-reel audio player atop the wooden HiFi cabinet we were never allowed to touch. The overhead light was bright but hazy due to clouds of cigarette smoke floating in the air.

My seven-year-old brain registered that the party was in full swing. The table, currently serving as a bar, displayed quite a selection of Seagram's 7 Crown Whiskey and 7UP bottles and half-empty glasses with lipstick marks on them.

Pressed close to my father's chest, I lifted my head toward the chatter and light. I recognized Uncle Frank, Aunt Marianne, and Mr. and Mrs. Plansky from across the street. They were all in various states of dishevelment—ties loosened, lipstick smeared, and jackets hanging off the edge of chairs, their smiles and mannerisms exaggerated by drink and the night's excitement. They were so engrossed in conversation they barely noticed me.

The annual Higganum-Haddam Fireman's Ball was the one night a year my dad splashed on some Old Spice, put in his teeth, donned a suit jacket and tie, and went out with my mom to dance and hoot and holler it up at the Three Oaks Inn.

Mom was always in a good mood on the day of the party. For weeks afterward, she'd often talk about what happened with one of her best friends over coffee or on the phone. I carefully overheard these conversations, and in asking other family members what they remembered, I've pieced together what may have happened.

I imagine that one night, while my parents and their friends had attended another Fireman's Ball, well after the band played their last song and were packing up, they got kicked out of the inn by the fire chief and his wife, only to continue the party with the promise of breakfast at our house.

The drivers caravanned behind one another that mile and a half to our house, slowly creeping up Jackon Hill on Route 81 and turning down the long, dark dirt road through the junkyard.

Inside the simple cedar-shingled house—built in stages over many years by my own Dad's hands with whatever materials he could scrounge up—this crazy group of mostly inebriated neighbors and family gathered around our large oak kitchen table because they weren't ready for the night to end.

Our house was the closest destination they could reach without getting pulled over, no matter how many drinks had been consumed. Once inside, Mom burst into action. "Who wants some eggies?" she asked shrilly, most likely slurring her words. She swayed back, almost falling over from the force of whipping open the Frigidaire door, giggling as she gathered eggs, milk, and bacon.

After eating and pouring another round or two of Seven and 7s, Dad tried to lure Mom out of her seat for another spin around the kitchen dance floor. She shooed him away, saying, "No, Bob," She gently rubbed her stocking feet, revealing red and purple spots where they had been squished into her "best" heels, worn once a year. "I really can't."

When it finally hit him that he needed a fresh dance partner, he'd turn around quickly and head upstairs to find me.

Me. He'd come for me.

I remember those precious moments as if they were yesterday, not fifty years ago: the almost queasy motion-sick feeling as I stretched my head away from him as we danced. I felt the air and force of our movement whirling around me as if I were on the merry-go-round juxtaposed by the solid security of my father holding me tight.

In that moment, we were the only two people in the room. I was Cinderella at the ball, feeling light as I floated across the floor, my tiny, bare feet dangling near his waist as he held me tight. Our fingers intertwined as we twirled and spun to the music. We'd laugh as he tried to sing the song to me but clearly didn't know all the words. Dad had a spectacular voice—deep, clear, and on-pitch. We didn't hear it often, but it soothed me. My face was so close to his that I could hear that clicky sound his fake bright white teeth made as they moved inside his mouth.

The following morning, I'd wake to wonder if it was all just some fantastically wonderful dream. And then, sometime late that afternoon, Dad would come out of his room sleepy and bleary-eyed, seeking a cup of black coffee. He would look at me and wink as he turned to my mom and say, "That was some night, wasn't it?"

I smiled, thinking, *Yes, it sure was.*

Magic

"OH, IT'S YOU," SHE SAID AS SHE OPENED THE DOOR TO SEE ME STANDING THERE ON the cement floor of the front porch that smelled like cats. I walked in, a bit sweaty and dusty from my trek through the junkyard to get to her house. She sighed when she noticed I was carrying my "runaway" bag (containing a few essentials, including a cellophane-wrapped Hostess cake, book, and some underwear) and said, grinning," "Looks like I've got a guest for the night. Come on in, and you can tell me what happened." Closing the door, she motioned for me to sit at the table. "I'll make us some tea, okay?"

When I was a child, I ran away to Grandma Watson's house, my father's mom, who lived at the bottom of the hill on the far side of the junkyard. Her house was my escape hatch. I was probably mad at Maddy or feeling the weight of the world's many injustices and needed an escape. Once I could ride my bike on the road, that became my escape. But while I was still young, I'd grab my bag, fill it with what I felt I needed, take it out our front door, and run. Run as if my life was in danger. Run because I needed to move. Run because I felt I would die if I didn't.

In the summer, it was dry, dusty, and hot as I followed that road, pumping my arms for extra propulsion on the dirt road that snaked down the hill through the main part of the junkyard. I ran around various car frames and piles of rusted-out debris. Eventually, the road—if you can call it that, as some parts of it were more like a path—took me through the trees, past the old garage with broken windows that sometimes Dad's "friends" stayed in, and to the left was the house Grandfather Watson built after losing a much larger home to debtors during the Depression. Occasionally, along the way to Grandma's, I'd make a pit stop to explore a car or truck I hadn't seen yet—flipping the seats and car mats looking for coins or forgotten treasures in the glove box.

Each car had its unique smell. Sometimes, it was a stale, musty air, sharing its emptiness and uselessness. Often, I'd try to imagine what the previous owners were like based on leftover smells and other evidence I'd found. I'd envision chain-smoking rough and tough guys if I noticed an ashtray full of cig butts and the familiar smell of smoke from the stained upholstery. Or a sweet young woman, probably a secretary or nurse, by the color of the car—metallic blue or deep maroon—and the fact I found a cardboard Christmas tree-shaped air-refresher still swinging from the rearview mirror filling up the junker with its fake pine or sweet floral scent.

Grandma Watson always had her hair pinned up in a tight circular bun with a few silver hairs escaping confinement to softly frame her weathered, wrinkled, and determined face. Dad had her nose—the one that looks a little bit too big for your face but still crinkled along with their eyes when they smiled.

Grandma Watson's voice could be gruff and sometimes sharp. I liked being with her. You always knew where you stood. She would give me "jobs" to do while I was there. "Laurie, shuck the corn." "Laurie, feed the cats." "Laurie, carry this to the junk pile out back." Life was predictable and structured in her little house by the pond.

She was a great listener and didn't say much beyond offering instructions for my tasks. She didn't have to. I babbled on and on about anything and everything while she listened calmly and quietly. I think she smiled, but it was hard to notice if that was what she was doing as I don't remember her having teeth.

Her face and posture said so much. She'd had a hard life, and it showed. Her back was constantly bent—getting worse as she got older.

She had raised nine children; Dad was the third youngest. She had lost a few, and she and Grandpa had to give up the family home to the bank during the Depression.

I didn't know Grandpa Watson very well, as he had died years earlier when I was a baby. No one talked about it. We weren't close to all our aunts, uncles, and cousins in the Watson clan. Despite most of them living fairly close, we never saw them. I never understood why, but it had something to do with a family argument between Dad and some of his siblings.

I loved Grandma's kitchen. It was ancient, with cracked black-and-white checkerboard linoleum floor tiles and a large old stove that you had to put wood in to use. She even had an icebox that, at one time, used blocks of ice to keep the food compartment cold. Now that she had an actual fridge, the old icebox overflowed with odd pieces of paper, mail, and magazines.

Sometimes we'd get a special treat. Grandma Watson would slather Wonder Bread slices with butter and sprinkle white sugar on them. Yum. Sometimes we'd take the trek to Grandma's to request that treat specifically. While we usually had a cardboard carton of some Hostess product at home, Dad got a kick out of the fact we'd trek to her house to ask for those sandwiches. Years later, Dad told us that was what he'd eat when they couldn't afford cookies, cake, or ice cream. He hated that "dessert." But, to us, it was the greatest!

One time, when I slept over, I was sneaking a peek through Grandma's slightly open bedroom door and caught her in her nightly bedtime routine. In a faded flowery night dress, she was facing away from me, looking into a worn mirror, carefully unpinning her bun to release a cascade of long silver strands of hair, almost reaching the bottom of the chair she was sitting in. She looked like a fairy queen with that mane of silver hair, slowly brushing it, making some strands electrify and rise in the air. I wanted to reach out and touch it so badly. But it felt like a private moment, so I crept away and never saw it down again. Each morning, she'd be in the kitchen with it all back up in a tight bun. I wish I had told her how lovely it was. I wish I had been brave enough to ask her to wear it down. I wish I had told her how magical she was to me.

Grandma lived in the small, modest house at the bottom of the junkyard that Grandpa Watson had built himself. Dad had done the same, building our home shingle-by-shingle in stages beside the trailer where we lived until the house was completed in the junkyard.

Grandma's house was a modest one-story house with a stone foundation built from smooth stones found in the creek behind it. It was one story of shingles, peeling white paint, a few square windows framed by dark green broken shutters, and trim. It overlooked a small pond we loved. It was magical and the destination of many of our adventures in all seasons. In early spring, we'd be environmental scientists carefully monitoring the amoeba-like pollywogs as they grew to tiny tadpoles darting every which way. Eventually, they became the frogs that liked to sun themselves on top of lily pads or rest partially submerged next to logs where turtles lay stretched out on top in a row.

In winter, we'd skate there with the neighbor kids, sometimes in the dark with just the flood lamp from the house porch casting a narrow band of light that we'd skate in and out of for hours. I remember sitting on the bank, warming our hands around mugs of Swiss Miss cocoa my Aunt Claire made for us.

One winter, I thought our pet dog—Mistress Brandy—was sad because she couldn't join the skating fun. I almost broke her little legs when I strapped ice skates onto her paws and tried to get her to skate with us. Another time, inspired by a story about Eskimos and dog sledding I had read in school, I wanted to tie her to our sled so she could pull us around, but she kept sliding away. I don't remember whose idea it was to take our Radio Flyer sleds to the top of the snow bank near the garage and bomb down, only to slide and laugh uncontrollably once we hit the ice on the pond. I can still feel the fear of imminent danger and hear our giggles as we climbed the hill to do it again.

That's also the same pond where I went fishing with my older cousin, who was visiting from Vermont so he could "teach" me how to fish. All set up, I masterfully threaded the squiggly worm on the hook. As he began to demonstrate how to cast the line, he requested that I step back. Then he flung the pole backward and caught my head instead of a fish. Several people had to hold me steady enough to get the hook out of my skull. Mom said it was good I had thick hair as I'm sure it still covers up a nasty scar.

Grandma's house wasn't far away, but it felt like we were in another world. It was peaceful and quiet and allowed us to be kids—not junk-yard kids—just kids.

One Dollar and Seventy-Nine Cents

I STOOD BEFORE THE BARBIE CLOTHES DISPLAYED IN BRADLEES DEPARTMENT
Store and dreamed. There they were: transparent plastic hard shells
containing the most fantastic collection of tiny clothes and fashion
accessories lined up on their pegs—taunting me.

There were so many to choose from, I couldn't decide. One included
a super-sparkly pink dress with ruffles, matching white plastic boots, and
even an open-and-close purse. I really liked the slumber party set: turquoise
PJs—short-short bottoms with a matching top; fuzzy blue slippers, a sleeping bag (with a coordinating pillow), and a diary that opened for real.

I had quite a few Barbie dolls at home—usually in various states of
undress on the bathroom floor, recuperating from our bath or positioned
in their makeshift townhome, which I constructed by taping several
empty shoe boxes to make an up- and downstairs. My Skipper, Malibu
Lifeguard Barbie, and Professional Secretary Barbie already had a pretty
full and fabulous wardrobe.

My mom was a master seamstress who made most of our clothes,
including my Barbie outfits. My heart warms, and my eyes hurt when
I think about how she took time and oh so much effort to make me
miniature outfits using teeny-tiny paper Simplicity patterns or eyeballing
my Barbies' favorite outfits to create her own patterns out of tissue paper.

Today, I'd give anything to touch those miniature fashionista
creations by my designer mom—especially the pale-yellow wool jacket

with a matching dress that matched the one I wore for Easter the year she made all five of us kids outfits for the holiday.

For my Barbies—the sky was the limit as long as the fabric remnant basket was full. She made sophisticated satin party dresses, wide-legged pants, and long maxi skirts—several with miniature metal zippers expertly sewn in. Although my Barbies were clothed in custom couture of quality fabrics, that human desire for something "new" and "shiny" drove me to covet those synthetic sparkly dresses in the plastic sleeves. Go figure.

On Saturday mornings, my well-coiffed grandmother Josephine—my mom's mother—had a standing wash-and-set appointment. Before this, Grandma had Grandpa do her hair at their own salon. But after they sold it and Grandpa passed away, Grandma had to find a salon that met her standards for her weekly appointment. She would travel to the nearby town of Middletown on Saturday mornings. Unlike our two-traffic-light town of Higganum—one light blinked, the other changed color—Middletown was a city offering retail and entertainment amenities, including a movie theater, Woolworth's, Pizza Palace, and Bradlees.

Some Saturdays, my grandmother would let me go with her. I felt so special, plopping into the back of the 1961 red Cadillac convertible. I loved having the whole back seat to myself. I imagined being chauffeured by a driver, although I never told her that.

Grandma Josephine hummed to music from the push button radio on the dash, occasionally selecting different stations with her manicured fingers. She'd smile at me as she glanced in the rearview mirror, adjusting it to see my face beaming from the white leather back seat.

After the ride, we'd grab something to eat at the Woolworth's luncheonette. Sometimes, she'd order the special, which varied, and I always got a grilled cheese with crinkle-cut fries. Then, she'd go into Jimmy's Beauty Salon for her appointment, and I'd sit on the pink and turquoise vinyl-covered chairs that always stuck to my legs no matter the temperature. Sometimes, I'd read a book from the library or pretend to read while listening to the ladies chat about things I didn't understand.

One afternoon at the Bradlees department store after the appointment, I'd gravitated to the Barbie aisle. Those coveted fashion sets cost a whopping dollar and seventy-nine cents, yet I usually found a way to ask her for one. I really, really, really wanted one. They were unlike the clothes my mom made. The allure of those fashions created the possibility of great dates, parties, and adventures my Barbies could experience if only they had the right outfit—the one that came in the plastic clamshell case. I just had to have them.

"Maybe," (which we all knew meant "no") Grandma would say as she gently placed the outfit back on its peg. So often, the words "we can't afford that" would accompany a similar request to my mom, so I assumed economics was also behind the "maybe" from my grandmother.

Grandmother and I would meander hand-in-hand through the store, ending up in the book section. She'd peruse the adult books and sometimes flip through *Life* magazines while I gravitated to the collection of Nancy Drew—my favorite super sleuth. Hardcover Nancy Drew books were two dollars, and after Grandma made our purchases, I usually walked out of the store with a new ND mystery in the paper Bradlees bag tucked under my arm.

As a child, I figured since we couldn't afford the Barbie outfits, they must have been more expensive than the books. I don't remember how old I was when I figured this out, but I eventually did the math. Although Grandmother Josephine died when I was still young, I'd like to think she would have smiled at how her two-dollar book purchases paid off as my love of reading shaped the storyteller and writer I am today.

Big Sis

EVERYONE NEEDS A BIG SISTER. WITH BLONDE HAIR FRAMING A ROUND FACE AND blue eyes almost as big as her heart, Cindy was mine.

Six years older, she would sled and ice skate with us down at Grandma's pond and come along for the ride in the old school bus from time to time. She'd play "house" with us in the woods near the brook. Cindy, Maddy, and sometimes Jack and I would create elaborate homes by rearranging rocks and tree stumps as furniture and sweeping the earth with Mom's broom (much to her displeasure because the next time she'd grab it to use it in our actual home, the floors must have been left dirtier after she swept). In our forest homes, we'd carefully outline where the kitchen and bedrooms would be and act out how we thought a typical family lived.

When we played house with Cindy, she was always the mom.

Later, when she could drive, she'd bring us all over town, sometimes running errands for Mom. Other times, we'd go out for a ride, radio blaring, wind whipping our hair from the open window.

Cindy was quiet but did more for me (and us all) than I ever realized. She didn't announce to the world what she carefully did behind the scenes. But like most of the girls in our town, she married just out of high school at the age of eighteen.

Then she had her own real "house" we could visit. Her house was tidy and filled with matching kitchen towels and mitts, shiny pots and pans, and plates and cups that weren't chipped. I wonder if her heart was as hopeful as mine the moment I crossed the welcome mat at her door.

I remember making an apple pie at her house. I don't know if Cindy or her mother-in-law taught me how to roll out the dough on her clean kitchen counter, but I remember the lesson: "Laurie, now we want to roll it into the shape of the earth like this. Not the shape of Africa." Later, I taught my own girls to roll pie dough using the same instructions.

Warm and spicy memories of making apple and pumpkin pies at Cindy's swirl in my mind even today. She'd let us take a warm pie from the oven home to the junkyard, allowing me to feel and taste her love long after I'd left her.

Cindy had escaped the junkyard, but the difficulties of life followed her. Her wish for a "normal" life with her husband did not go as she had hoped. After a few years of difficulty in her first marriage, Mom came to her rescue and pulled her back home.

She eventually married her second and current husband, James, the son of one of Dad's junkyard acquaintances, and went on to have two children. Cindy is a wonderful mom. It was as if she was made for the role. She raised her family in a home filled to the brim with love, care, and most definitely homemade pies.

Despite the many hardships Cindy dealt with—many of which I bet I have no idea about to this day—she was always and is still the best friend, mom, and big sis anyone could hope for. I melt into her love when she greets me, heart open and arms stretched wide for a hug.

Junkyard Snow Globe

"IT'S SNOWING!" EXCLAIMED AN EXCITED MADDY AS SHE SCRAPED THE FROST OFF
the inside of our bedroom window with her fingers to watch big fat flakes
float by or hit the window and dissolve.

Snow was one thing that made the junkyard look nice. A new cover of
the white stuff hid all the ugliness and brought a freshness the real thing
never had. Looking at the snowy landscape outside our window, I felt
a quiet sense of calm and appreciation as I saw white shapely hills and
valleys—not tire and hubcap piles or rusted-out profiles of cars and trucks.
As the sun sparkled off the snow, it actually looked pretty and inviting!

I imagined the junkyard encased in one of those snow globes you
can get at tourist attractions like Niagara Falls or New York City. It
would be cool to shake it quickly to make my surroundings sparkle and
magically transform as the snow specs fell softly, making the scene look
shiny, pretty, and calm. Seeing snowfall blanketing the junkyard had a
similar effect.

Despite the joy I felt at the prospect of a fun and thrilling afternoon
sledding and possibly hot chocolate afterward, I pulled the covers up
to my chin as it was cold inside our bedroom. A happy feeling slowly
warmed me from the inside. We had been waiting for this moment since
the leaves fell. We had a plan.

A few hours later, after finally finding matching boots that fit and
bundled up in our snowsuits with mismatched mittens church ladies had
knit us, Maddy, Jack, and I were outside with the neighbors—Kat and
Terry Plansky—ready to implement "the plan."

Each of us grabbed hubcaps from the pile—carefully selecting those with a good bowl shape, occasionally discarding those that weren't quite right. We were seeking a custom shape that gave us ample room for our bottoms, allowing some space to put our hands on at least one edge. It took some trial and error to find the right one.

Holding our hubcap of choice, we trudged up the big hill of our driveway, digging our snow boots in for extra traction with each step up until we gathered breathlessly at the top crest to survey the course below. Although we were looking forward to sledding down with our hubcaps all morning—now, at the moment of truth—the view from the steep hill gave us pause. We looked at each other, wide eyes popping out from under hats and hoods.

Jack was the mastermind of today's sledding adventure. Although he was the youngest, he often coaxed us into some risky activity once he was old enough to pressure us to comply. It was hard to resist his crooked smirk, knowing so much more was happening in his brain. My little brother may have been small in stature, but he was always big on ideas,

His brilliant idea today was to tie all of our hubcaps together to make a chain so we could become a bobsled team. A discussion ensued on how to implement it. How do we attach the ropes to each hubcap? Where can we find rope without bothering anyone in the garage—thus alerting them of our plan? What do we do if a car suddenly comes down the driveway? Would our proposed method of steering—previously discussed while we were formulating our plan a few weeks earlier (moving our weight around from side to side, hoping the hubcap would respond by moving in that direction)—work if we were tied together?

"I don't know," said Maddy, frowning. "I think we might crash." Maddy was hesitant as usual, her logical brain working out all the possible issues in seconds. I usually erred on the side of safety but was always up for figuring out our options to safely implement one of Jack's wild and quirky ideas.

It's funny to think of this now as years later, Maddy became a bit more daring later in life while I was risk-averse, always looking for a way to control any outcome. Jack? Thankfully, he'd always be our own Evel Knievel, a waif of a sandy-haired boy, always grinning, ready for whatever we'd demand. Whether that be making him taste (and eat) our mud pie or cake creations or having Jack be the student who was always in trouble when we played school (Maddy or I always being the teacher). Jack was our little bro, quirky and ready to try anything.

But for this challenge, I couldn't see how we could control our make-shift sleds except to suggest, "We can always just jump off if we feel we are out of control." Ah, that was my other magic power—when control wasn't possible, I was always looking for a safe escape.

Ultimately, we got settled in our individual silver saucer sleds and eventually slid down the hill—out of control—but laughing all the way. Some of us experienced an unexpected thrill as our hubcaps occasionally spun as we gained speed and momentum. Once on the bottom, Jack searched for rope, which he found in the shed. We all climbed back to the top, lining up behind one another, with Jack in the lead and each of us holding a piece of the rope since we couldn't figure out how to attach them.

We counted down as if we were a rocket at liftoff. In seconds, we were careening down, semi-connected. We didn't anticipate that due to our varying weights and heights and some of us pushing off with more force than others, our hubcap Congo line veered "off course" as we slid down at different speeds. This also jerked some of us who were purposely trying to go slower.

The result? I let go while Maddy didn't. The rest of us tumbled off one after another in differing directions while our "sleds" continued careening down the hill. At the same time, Maddy and Jack slid sideways and ended up hitting a tree down an embankment to the side of the driveway.

They weren't hurt. Just stunned. When a few of us reached them—laughing—Maddy got mad and stormed down the hill to go inside. Jack just shook the snow off and said, "Let's do that again." The four of us spent a bit more time trying various configurations and eventually got tired and cold and went inside for Swiss Miss packets of instant cocoa—yes, with the mini marshmallows floating on top.

Running

HIS LONG, LANKY BODY WAS BUILT FOR IT. HIS SKINNY TORSO STRETCHED FROM the waistband of his running shorts while long muscular legs appeared as alien appendages with minds of their own.

He had a lot of reasons to run. I knew that feeling—that feeling of desperately needing to run away. I guess we all did. But Ryan knew what he was running toward.

Ryan was on the track and cross-country teams all four years of high school. Mom would take us to as many of his meets as our current junker car could get us to.

She'd round up us kids to get into the car, and despite putting the pedal to the metal, we'd still pull into the Xavier High School parking lot just in time to hear the gun go off in the distant field. Run-walking toward where the action was, we'd see the line of various colored tanks surging forward and scattering like colored bits of confetti in the wind.

We may not have spotted him at the start of a race, but we'd sure figure out which runner he was at the finish. We'd see his arms pumping, red face sporting a determined look, and nerdy glasses foggy yet secured in place by a wet headband spanning across the back of his head. Our voices were louder than most. Our pitch would rise and reach a crescendo just as he would be a blur running past. He was almost always one of the first to cross the finish line. In fact, Ryan broke numerous school records in his high school career and neglected to come in first only once or twice!

I was proud of my big brother. He was going somewhere. I didn't learn he was my half-brother until much later in life. In retrospect, I should have figured it out by the heated arguments Mom and Dad would get in whenever Ryan or Cindy needed something that had a dollar sign attached to it—or when one of them acted like teenagers typically do.

Maddy, Jack, and I often "got away with murder," according to Cindy, while she and Ryan got the brunt of Dad's bad mood and temper. Yet, I still have muscle memory of the impact of Dad's "boot" or leather belt strap on my behind, so I don't think we got off scot-free.

Ryan was born "by appointment" in a Brooklyn hospital on September 9, 1952. Mom told us she paced back and forth on the sidewalk in front of the hospital, smoking cigarette after cigarette, too nervous to go to the maternity ward.

According to her story, eventually, a nurse came down, saw a very pregnant woman on the sidewalk, verified it was Mom, and beckoned her inside so she could keep her appointment to give birth to her baby.

It was common in the forties and fifties to arrange to give birth just as if you were making a hair appointment. Mom said as long as your doctor had determined your baby was "cooked enough," you would show up at a pre-set date and time. Many mothers would select their children's birthdays this way. She explained that you'd be put to sleep by being given "twilight gas," only to wake up hours later not remembering anything about the birth but groggily holding your baby as if a stork had delivered it!

Recalling this story of Ryan's birth, I wonder why his dad isn't in it. He is missing from the story, just as he was in most of Ryan and Cindy's life.

I don't know why I never figured out we had different dads. It just didn't come up. We never talked about Dad being a "stepdad" versus their "real' dad or anything like that.

Given our financial difficulties, Dad may have resented that he took on the responsibility and economic burden of raising and parenting them. Yet Dad did step up to the task and even asked Ryan if he wanted to be adopted.

According to Ryan, while he was only six years old, Dad sat him down and offered to make Ryan his official "son" on paper. He said that no matter what he chose, Ryan would always be his son, yet he might want to keep his original last name just in case his real Dad would leave him some money someday. Dad was looking out for Ryan's best interest and realized that perhaps Ryan's best chance to get an inheritance was from his real dad—and not him.

Fast forward decades, and it was Ryan who delivered a beautiful—and funny—tribute to Dad at his funeral. While I don't remember his exact words, I do recall Ryan getting emotional at the end (which was a rarity for his introverted demeanor), saying, "I had a choice of fathers. And I chose the right one."

I remember thinking about Ryan admitting that Dad was his father rather than his birth father. I thought back to Mom. I had no idea how Mom felt about her ex-husband not being involved in his children's childhood. She never talked about it. When she met my dad, I imagine she may have thought she needed to find a father for her young children, and he fit the bill.

When I was a teenager pondering big subjects like love, lust, sex, and the mystery of relationships, I would naturally wonder about Dad and Mom. Our family was not affectionate; I don't remember seeing Mom and Dad hug, kiss, or even hold hands. And I have very few memories of them holding or physically comforting us kids—except when we might have fallen or been injured.

I recall laughter and fun and, unfortunately, fear, which permeated most of my childhood memories—but that is for other reasons. After Mom died after being ill for years, I remember seeing a soft sadness in Dad's azure eyes. He looked relieved, tired, and lost.

I have also wondered if Ryan's real dad—who I later learned was Ryan Senior—helped pay for Xavier High School, the private Catholic school where Ryan was a track star, or if he was the recipient of a scholarship. Maybe Grandma and Grandpa Martinez pitched in, or Dad and Mom scraped up the cash.

Xavier was a private Catholic school in Middletown and had a much more diverse student body than our local high school. Cindy attended a public high school in Middletown.

Running came naturally to Ryan. A few months after high school graduation, he continued to run.

The plan—if Ryan and his friends even had one—was to travel across the country, stopping wherever they wanted; sleeping at campgrounds, rest stops, and roadsides; and eventually ending up in California, where Ryan Senior lived. Ryan wanted to get to know his dad. Mom didn't understand it and didn't want Ryan to go. "You'll just be disappointed, Ryan," she warned. "He's the same asshole now as he was when I left him." Ryan, incited by his desire to know his dad, retorted, "Mom, I just want to find out for myself."

So he did.

A few months later—Ryan and his buddies, having been freed from their Catholic high school's hair length restrictions and sporting sported ponytails and new-growth scruffy beards—piled essentials such as sleeping bags, mess kits leftover from boy scout camp, boxes full of food that didn't require refrigeration, marijuana, and whatever cash they had saved into a VW van and sped out of our dirt driveway leaving behind a cloud of dust.

Years later, Ryan would tell his kids tales of almost being arrested by suspicious southern cops—skeptical of what these long-haired twenty-something northerners were doing in their county—stopping the van, ultimately unable to find a reason to arrest or fine them. Or the strangers they picked up along the route and unique but certainly illegal "camping" spots they spent the night at.

Ryan settled in California and attended college, eventually gaining a computer science degree and discovering that Mom was again right. His dad was indeed an asshole.

Scrap Metal Shaman

HOLIDAY MIRACLES HAPPEN. MOM AND DAD SOMEHOW MANAGED TO PUT A TURKEY with all the trimmings on the table at Thanksgiving and tons of gifts under the Christmas tree. During the cold winter months, the number of strangers sitting around the kitchen table dipped with the temperatures bringing unusual peace and stability to our home. The junkyard was a magnet for vagabonds and drifters. Dad would often offer some strangers a cup of coffee in our kitchen. After hearing their hard-luck story, Dad would invite them to stay a bit longer to work off the cost of a part they desperately needed or to make some cash so they could move on somewhere else.

No matter who was with us, we did our best to make the season festive. Mom crocheted pot holders, afghans, and vests. At the same time, we kids made snow angels, went skating on Grandma Watson's pond, and almost killed ourselves sledding down the icy steep hill, making quick lifesaving maneuvers to avoid colliding with the pile of hubcaps.

Christmas Eve was the one of the few nights of the year that Dad would shave, put his teeth in, don a button-down shirt, and join us in making his annual appearance at the candlelight Christmas Eve services at St. John's Episcopal Church. While Dad rarely went, the rest of us were church regulars. Mom served on the church council, and us kids often received the perfect attendance award for Sunday school, especially since Mom was also a Sunday school teacher.

On that crisp Christmas Eve, Dad was sitting when he should be standing and vice versa. His voice reverberated deep in his throat as he sang loudly. His surprisingly beautiful alto voice harmonized with the chorus, making even "Silent Night" seem like a jolly tune. One year, when the candle he held somehow ignited its own Dixie cup holder, we had to stomp it out in the pew, adding an impromptu percussion beat to the congregation's rendition of "The Little Drummer Boy."

Mom, regaining her composure once she realized the church wasn't going up in flames, glanced around to see if any of her friends had noticed. All of us kids exchanged grins behind our own lit Dixie cups. Dad winked at us and kept singing.

He always got a bit of the devil in him at Christmas. My older brother and sister—Ryan and Cindy—shared a story of Dad at Christmas that has become a bit of family lore. Apparently, one December, Dad rigged a plastic lit-up Santa complete with a mini sleigh and a glowing red-nosed Rudolph high up in a tree close to the trailer to look like it was flying through the air.

I remember none of this. I was just a baby. But Cindy and Ryan remember being snug in their bed, the glow of Santa shining in their window, dreaming of his impending visit.

Later, they were awoken by the sounds of a few shots and what appeared to be a scuffle on the roof. Dad had had one too many Seven and 7s while Mom was wrapping gifts. He grabbed his shotgun and climbed onto the roof of the trailer. "I've gotcha, Santa!" he shouted after firing his gun. "Now, you better take off before I grab everything you've got!" He stomped the roof and fired again. Terrified, Cindy and Ryan peeked out the window just in time to see Santa disappear from the tree line. Dad had shot "Santa's light out"—the lights he had put up earlier.

Dad wove a convincing tale about how he grabbed as many gifts as he could from Santa's sleigh (many of them intended for other kids in the neighborhood) and was able to shoot down one of the reindeer before Santa escaped. He said his plan was to get the sleigh—for scrap metal, of course—but Santa was sly and got away.

In the coming weeks, while eating overcooked venison—a staple in our home due to the generosity of our Vermont cousins who were avid hunters—Dad commented that we were eating reindeer meat scored from his roof-top run-in with Santa.

How Cindy and Ryan could have eaten what they thought was Rudolph, I don't know. They later told me they were embarrassed to get on the bus that year after winter school break for fear that Dad had ruined Christmas for all the neighborhood kids.

The only way I can justify this behavior is that perhaps Dad thought he was being funny and clever, yet this was one case where it was more hurtful than humorous.

Mom couldn't do anything when Dad was like this. Dad was either angry or completely silly. He would have one of these light bulb moments—something like shooting Santa—which he somehow thought was a harmless practical joke, ultimately not landing on others the way he thought it would. Or he'd be plain old silly, doing this silly shuffle dance on table tops or making a public display of taking his teeth out in front of guests, proudly displaying a toothless grin as he rested his smile next to his plate.

Mom was powerless when Dad was on a roll. I imagine that over the years, what had attracted her to him—being a prankster and quick-witted—was what wore her down most. I could hear her sigh and noticed her pursed lips as she stuffed her anger and disappointment. She had no choice and went along with his shenanigans, picking up the pieces afterward.

To know and love Dad as we did—you accepted him for who he was—full of contradictions and unique as a snowflake. Underneath the tough and wacky exterior, he was a good man.

Dad was a World War II vet and a steel worker for years, building bridges and working high in the air, until he got "blackballed" from the Steelworkers Union for having a reputation for being "hot-headed" and "quick-tempered." Starting the junkyard just kind of happened.

Grandpa Watson had a small gas station up the hill from the house he built. He started it during the Depression to make some cash, figuring everyone needed gas, and it was a long way into town to the next station. Dad was gifted mechanically and occasionally would make extra cash fixing someone's broken car at the makeshift gas station. He began to collect used cars for spare parts, and as the cars multiplied, the junk-yard was born.

Dad was a scrap metal shaman. A psychic with dirt under his finger-nails and a bad temper, he practiced Transcendental Meditation, and read mystic poetry and books on spiritualism late into the night.

Yes. Dad was a conundrum.

He could be a ruthless son of a bitch who'd grab his gun, run outside in his sagging Fruit of the Looms, and shoot into the air to scare off the poor bastards who snuck in to steal from us. But he was also a gifted energy healer. At night, when I couldn't sleep because of a toothache or tummy ache, he'd gently hold me while taking away the pain as he did a "healing" so I could go back to sleep.

He proudly attended my school concerts and theatrical performances and told us knock-knock jokes as well as limericks—"There once was a man from Nantucket whose cock was so long he could suck it"—that we never repeated to Mom.

Dad was intelligent, handsome, and charismatic, yet a mystery to most who met him.

When my husband's cousin John met Dad at a roadside McDonald's en route to go camping together, he couldn't believe he was the same man my husband Rich had described: a psychic who found lost children and stayed up until dawn reading spiritual texts. John told Rich he expected a man in white flowing robes surrounded by light. Instead, there was Dad, wearing a worn blue work shirt with the name Bob embroidered above the pocket, chain-smoking cigarettes and drinking coffee. Dad looked up, grinning his toothless grin, and asked, "What the fuck took you so long?"

Slasher Mom

WHEN I WALKED INTO THE HOUSE FROM TAKING THE LATE BUS HOME FROM HIGH school drama club, she was sitting at the worn oak kitchen table, elbows bent, head in hands, despair swirling in the clouds of cigarette smoke surrounding her.

Looking at me as I plopped my overflowing book bag in a chair next to her, Mom sighed, exhaling stale, warm breath. Taking one last drag on what was left of her cigarette, she crushed the butt with purpose among the others in the overflowing ashtray.

As I was opening up the fridge on automatic pilot, my hypnotic state staring into the fridge was interrupted by Mom suddenly straightening up as if she had decided something. "Up for an adventure?" she asked.

"Guess so," I shrugged.

She walked to the kitchen, reached up to open the top cabinet door, took out something, put it in her purse, grabbed her keys, and said, "Let's go." Minutes later, I was seated in the front passenger side of the latest junker she was driving, and we peeled out of the driveway, leaving a cloud of dust in our wake.

I watched her drive, noticing her dark, short, wiry hair was a mess. Her hazel eyes were rimmed in red as if she had been crying. Her skin didn't look as it did in the framed photo we had of her when she graduated high school—all rosy and fresh. If worn out and defeated was a color, that was her current skin shade.

Was that anger or determination I could feel as she gripped the steering wheel? Whatever it was, we were heading toward it. Turning away,

I looked out the window and watched the trees blur, feeling the fresh air on my face washing away any concern I had.

"We have just enough time before we have to get Maddy at gymnastics," she said as if she were talking to no one. She gunned it as we hit the ramp onto the highway. I could tell she was figuring something out in her head. "Aunt Shirley and Uncle Ty will return Jack from drum practice later tonight, so we have just enough time."

"Time to do what?" I asked, wishing we were heading to the mall or getting a slice of pizza. "Where are we going, Mom?"

Her hands gripped the steering wheel tighter. "To HER house."

At thirteen, I was no stranger to drama, anger, and revenge. The fights between Mom and Dad had increased in frequency over the past few months. I had heard mention of "her" but had no idea who she was. I didn't want to know. Yet the closer we got to "her," the knot in my stomach grew because I knew I would soon find out.

As the exit signs whirled past us, a heavy, expectant silence settled between us. It was thick with anticipation, though of what I wasn't sure. Eventually, we exited and drove down a few streets. Mom seemed to know where she was going, but we turned into a neighborhood I had never seen.

Mom eased the car past a small white house and parked just beyond the mailbox. She shut the engine off and took a drag from her cigarette. We sat there for a few moments as she glared out the window. She seemed to be taking in the view—the lawn, the shrubbery, the small but relatively well-kept home. Then she zeroed in on the blue car sitting in the driveway. Mom put out her cigarette and grabbed something from her purse. "I'll be right back," she said.

I saw my mother walk toward the driveway of the house. Something silver flashed. What was in her hand? I tried to focus on the object in her hand as she crouched and moved with slow, intentional steps toward the house. Wait. Was that the knife we sometimes use to carve the turkey when the electric carver was on the fritz? What was she doing???

My heart pounded as I watched her walk up the driveway toward the house. In a panic, I held my breath. My fingers gripped the door handle, and I was about to jump out to stop her when she approached the car parked in front of the garage door attached to the house. I saw her duck down beside the car's passenger side.

Hidden from the view of the house and me, I stretched my neck just in time to watch her stab the front passenger tire several times with our carving knife until the air seeped out, and it was flat. She wiped her brow and repeated this to the back tire. As she ran back to the car, I saw the knife cut the air around her as if she were a wild woman and not my mom. I think she was laughing, but I could tell she was scared by her wide eyes.

Once inside our car, she slid the knife back into her purse. "Wow, that felt good," she panted out of breath.

Without missing a beat, she started up the car, did a U-turn, and a few minutes later, we were back on the highway.

As her breath—and my heart rate—began to normalize, we settled into a productive silence as we both were having inner conversations we couldn't yet voice out loud.

Who was this wild, impulsive woman sitting beside me? What did she just do? I'd never seen her like this. It scared me, but it also was exciting—like I was seeing Mom take action and do something for herself.

Mom broke the silence. "You know you can't tell anyone what we did, right?"

"You can count on me, Mom," I promised with a smirk. "It's our secret."

My mind continued to whirl with what-ifs and possible consequences. I wanted to ask questions but knew better. Instead, eventually, I rested my head on the back of the seat and watched her drive. I noticed her. She looked younger, happier, and lighter than she had earlier at the kitchen table. Her skin had a certain glow to it now.

I turned my focus inward and realized I was feeling something, too. What was this feeling? My heart felt full, puffed up almost. Pride. I felt proud I could be part of something so important to Mom. That I could do something for her. With her. I was her witness. I saw her staking her claim to something she thought she had lost. I felt her strength. Her strength became my strength. Our strength. It felt good.

She turned the radio up, and I rolled down my window. The radio was blaring, and the wind was whipping our hair. We drove back home. We felt free.

We never spoke about this to each other or anyone else, for that matter. It was our secret. It sat alongside so many other childhood secrets until now.

PART TWO

I Am Junk

The Almost Party

IT WAS SUPPOSED TO BE A PARTY, AND MOM AND I HAD PLANNED FOR A MONTH. What theme would it be? Barbies or Lucky Trolls? Colors? Would Mom make the cake, or could we special order a store-bought one that sported those ultra-sugary roses and came in a box with a see-through cellophane top so we could marvel at the perfectly formed cursive words that spelled out "Happy 8th Birthday, Laurie"?

I don't remember the specific details of this particular birthday with perfect clarity. While I think it was around age eight, I recall the sharp, cut-to-the-core pain it brought.

The junkyard was not the best location for entertaining except for our motley crew of regulars seated around the kitchen table—close friends and family or the eccentric, odd fellows Dad attracted. While parties were a rarity, we hosted some interesting family gatherings—particularly on holidays like Christmas Eve—and our birthdays.

Birthdays were celebrated by blowing up a few balloons and unrolling the recycled colored crepe paper banners scotch-taped together too many times but still providing a festive air—to be hung from the dusty hurricane kitchen light. Someone would whip up a "homemade" Betty Crocker mix chocolate cake—sporting homemade buttercream frosting—served oven to table in the same ancient beat-up aluminum rectangle cake pan. Of course, no birthday or special occasion went without our family's celebratory rituals, always including loud singing—in pretty good harmony—and ice cream.

Oh—and birthday presents! Mom was magical, and looking back now with the economic mind of an adult, I don't know how she managed to pull off getting us just what we wanted despite the dismal level of our bank account.

Mom, I imagine, wanted this birthday of mine to be remarkable. She had consoled me more than once over the past few years when invites were passed around at the school lunch table, and I didn't get one. I believe she felt the sting herself each time it happened to me and thus reasoned that perhaps we'd need to invite others to get an invite. So this year was the year she reluctantly agreed to let me have a real birthday party with friends.

We planned and schemed. Yes, we'd have party games! We purchased a pin-the-tail-on-the-donkey game with little tails you cut out of the cardboard box and unfolded to display a demonic-looking-yet-colorful painting of a sacrificial target mule.

I remember being nervous as I reached inside my lunch pail for the carefully addressed party invites I had done over the weekend in my best cursive. My heart beating faster, I carefully slid them across the lunch table to some of my best friends, who were all busy chatting and eating their peanut butter and fluff sandwiches. I was afraid they wouldn't notice them and throw them out with their cellophane wrappers and waxed paper, but a few smiled as they put them inside their lunch boxes, easing my anxiety. Hyperaware of those kids around us that I couldn't invite, I was careful to time it so I didn't offer up an invite in front of anyone I couldn't fit on the invite list. I solemnly vowed I would never cause anyone else to feel the familiar sharp sting of being left out.

Weeks earlier, when we had sat down to plan the party, Mom explained that the guest list had to be limited to the number of years I was to become. As I tried to calculate who I could include from my class, she said, "And I think when you turn double digits in a few years, you and your friends might be old enough for a sleepover. How does that sound?" I couldn't believe my luck—having a party this year and then being able to have a sleepover where I could spend that much time with my friends! My mind raced to imagine the intimate details we'd share in whispers while tucked into our sleeping bags.

Mom's voice interrupted my brief future dream, "Laurie, I'm afraid this year we will have to limit our invites because we don't have a lot of space. Okay?" Looking back, I guess the limit was most likely due to our party budget, but that didn't bother me then. I was hosting a birthday party!

The day of the party came. I put on a dress mom had made me—it was flowered cotton with a white Peter Pan collar and short sleeves. It was a bit too summery for the chilly early April weather—but I put it on anyway. I was so excited!

Mom and I gathered the party supplies, laid out the paper tablecloth with matching plates and cups, and blew up the balloons to hang above the table. We had even put together small goodie bags with candy and treats for our guests, and I reluctantly made sure there was one for Maddy and Jack.

Soon, Kat Plansky, our neighbor my age, came bopping up the hill and arrived with a gift in her hand. We both waited outside, watching pensively for a sign of other guests arriving.

I have no idea how long we sat there, waiting for a car to come with a guest inside. I don't know what we talked about or if I shared the mixed emotions I must have been feeling: the sinking feeling of having a party and no one coming.

Mom did break up time by delivering various birthday treats to us, including Cheez Doodles wrapped in festive napkins and red Hi-C punch splashing out of full birthday paper cups. We sipped in silence. Eventually, we came inside to sit at the nearly empty table filled with brightly colored place settings that sat empty.

Mom may have said something, but I don't remember. My family and Kat gathered around, and with Dad's solid singing voice joining in, sang "Happy Birthday." Mom lit the candles, and I dutifully blew them out. We ate the individual plastic cups of ice cream Mom had splurged on, and I opened Kat's gift and those that my mom had wrapped.

It didn't make sense to me. It was a party. Why didn't anyone come?

I felt an ache inside, deeper than a tummy ache. It hurt in a way I hadn't felt before. I clutched my stomach. Dad assumed I had eaten too much cake and tried to make me feel better by making funny faces at Kat and me.

Seeking to make sense of this situation, I thought we might have gotten the date wrong. Maybe my friends thought it was next Saturday? That there must have been some mistake? Who would miss a birthday party like this? I never voiced these questions, yet they remained inside for a long time. Everyone pretended everything was okay. Except it wasn't.

I felt alone, but looking back, I see how much I was loved, especially with Mom's extraordinary effort to make this birthday wonderful and friend-filled. There wasn't anything else she could have done. We lived in a junkyard that was no place for an eight-year-old's birthday party. Other moms and dads knew that. It's just that we didn't.

I never attempted to have another party at my house except for family parties and gatherings. Mom put on a lavish, amazing, sweet sixteen birthday party at St. James Church Hall, which was one of the most amazing parties I've ever had. I remember someone—maybe my boyfriend—gifted me a large, almost life-sized stuffed giraffe. It was a cool and unique gift I still remember vividly, along with the silver Speidel ID bracelet with my initials engraved that Mom gave me. I recently found that bracelet, tarnished but saved in an old jewelry box.

I never talked with Mom or Dad about my eighth birthday party, where no one bothered to come. I wonder what they felt, especially Mom. As a mom myself, I'm sure the sting of it was even sharper for her because she would have had occasions after that day to interact with perhaps some of the other parents, knowing they had a role in hurting her child.

I may have erased the hurt and embarrassment I felt when I returned to the school lunch table that Monday after my birthday weekend. I am sure I put on a fake smile and shared how wonderful the cake and all the gifts I received were. I'm sure I didn't mention it to my then "best friend" Robin, who didn't show.

I didn't know how to deal with all this messiness other than to do what I knew I could: pretend.

Pretending was my coping compass. Acting as if everything was just fine meant I didn't have to face what was really going on.

When I became a parent, I was determined to create a home where everyone was welcome. We often invited entire classes—especially when the kids were young—so that we would never be the cause of some small child not understanding why they weren't asked. I wanted our home to be where all the kids loved to hang out. I wanted to have a house where everyone felt "at home."

We hosted an epic holiday open house every year, complete with babysitters, kids' crafts, and yummy food and drink for all. One year, we hired a horse-drawn sleigh to take guests for a ride at nearby Sonnenberg Gardens.

Our eldest daughter, Liz, often gathered her friends after school at our house. We were within walking distance from both the middle and high school. Our wooded lot and sizable Victorian home became the setting for many films and plays Liz and her friends would create for school projects or just for fun. We'd host "screenings" and "performances" in our front room, complete with tickets and intermission.

My youngest daughter, Hannah, also loved hosting her friends and classmates at our house. She was the party planner extraordinaire. She loved orchestrating her events with elaborate themes requiring meticulous planning, invites, decor, and more.

I remember a murder mystery party she planned in middle school. Each guest had a character to play for the murder. It also required us to set up the murder scene, complete with the placement of an over-sized stuffed kitty slipper. Clues led her guests to the gruesome murder scene where she had sacrificed one of her fluffy slippers that looked like a stuffed animal. We filled the space where your foot would go with cold spaghetti and tomato sauce spilling out around the sides to resemble the murder victims' insides. It was her creative idea!

I also recall a lovely invite for a root beer–tasting party with "tasting cards" for attendees to rate the fizziness and flavor of the root beers served in my best crystal glasses.

Inclusion—with a capital "I"—became the mantra I wanted our daughters to understand, and they did. The intangible gift I gained from my eighth birthday was the importance of always being as inclusive as possible.

Birthdays would continue to be life lessons. My middle daughter Beck continued to teach me how vital acceptance was. The birthday themes she selected were mostly animal-themed and indisputably never pink or girly like her older sister. Beck always had more boys on her birthday invite list than girls. "Mom, the girls are just too much!" she'd say, exasperated. "When I'm with Mike and Daran, we get mad, but we say what we feel to get it over with and get back to playing quicker." It was simple. She didn't want the drama that accompanied girlfriends. As I think back on her logic, I smile at the truth of her words.

For Beck's tenth birthday, she was looking forward to hosting a sleepover like her sister Liz had when she turned "double digits." Rich and I had a behind-the-bedroom-door discussion because, again, most of Beck's friends were boys, and we were afraid the other families wouldn't let their boys stay for a sleepover at our house. We decided I would call the moms and explain, assuring them it would be an innocent sleepover, and we'd keep a close eye on the group. There was no need to worry. Some boys stayed long enough to get to change into their Teenage Mutant Ninja Turtle PJs and settle into their sleeping bags for movie time and left at 11 p.m. A few of Beck's closest friends—Daran and Mike, along with a few of the girls—slept over and were there in the morning, giggling at whispered secrets and gobbling up chocolate chip pancakes at a rate faster than we could flip them. They sat beside each other, sticky hands passing around the maple syrup and whipped cream. I can still hear the can squirting piles of whipped cream on top of those warm pancakes. They were besties, and it all worked out.

Inclusion is more than accepting others. It's about accepting who we are. As a child, I wanted to be included—and accepted—so much that I became amoeba-like, conforming to who I thought I needed to be in any situation. Beck knew who she was and pushed us to accept her. I wish I had given Beck—and all our daughters—even more space to show up as who they are. Inclusion does have a capital "I". . . it is about oneself, I know now.

Sometimes, the truth is a joy. Sometimes, truth is our greatest pain. Sometimes, it is our biggest lesson.

Strangers Around the Table

MY SISTERS AND BROTHERS AND I WOULD ENTER THE KITCHEN AT ANY TIME TO find various vagabonds sitting there. The six mismatched captain's chairs around the table were rarely empty. Most were men; many were strangers. All of them were chain-smoking, drinking Maxwell House out of chipped coffee mugs, and arguing or, as Mom would say, "having a heated conversation."

Whatever you want to call it, the conversation was always peppered with swear words uttered in various accents—most commonly fast-talking Italian (accompanied by lewd hand movements) or slow Southern drawls spoken with toothless smiles. These "heated conversations" would eventually hit a crescendo when someone's rough hand slammed on the table for added emphasis.

I was so used to the word "fuck" being used as an adjective, it didn't faze me when my dad exclaimed, "You are fucking beautiful!" upon seeing me descend the stairs from my bedroom in my yellow junior prom dress when I was sixteen years old. My eyes shone with pride. It was one of the most memorable compliments he had ever given me. His clear blue eyes crinkled a bit as his lips formed a toothless grin, taking all of me in.

Dad had much in common with our guests, as he was just as odd as they were. The strangers served a purpose as Dad needed cheap daytime labor because our Dad was a new-age vampire who stayed up all night reading Edgar Cayce books or meditating. He wouldn't even think of sleeping until the sun peeked through our threadbare curtains. The guys were more than happy to greet customers at 9 a.m. while Dad was fast asleep in bed. Thanks to Dad's big heart, many of these men entered our home as strangers but always left as friends.

Life among this motley crew was never dull. I never knew who would be at our table or what adventurer we might meet.

While I am sure I don't remember all the strange men who became temporary residents, I do recall a few specific characters seated around our kitchen table so often they could have had name plates on their chairs.

My favorite was Mike Love. He had a beard and long, straggly hair and wore tie-died apparel from his clothing line. His beat-up Volkswagen van sported colorful "Flower Power" and "Make Love, Not War" bumper stickers. At one time, the van was missing a window and, in its place, was a painted piece of cardboard that looked like a church-stained glass window. If nothing else, he was creative.

When he was in town, Mike Love lived above the old garage at the bottom of the junkyard. One year, he turned part of the garage into a candle-making business and made a heap of cash selling multicolored candles at fairs and music festivals. I have fond memories of Mike Love's kind and gentle demeanor. I was never afraid of him.

Mike Love was always calm—but I guess there was always a reason for this.

Dad would sit at the table and smoke pot when Mike Love was with us. He'd smoke a joint with him in front of us kids. I never gave it much thought. It just was what happened at my house.

Then there was Grub—or at least that's what we called him behind his back. Short, always needing a shower, his leathery face sprouted several weeks' scruff. He had curly dark hair matted with god-knows-what. His best features were perhaps his dark almond eyes, which within a millisecond, could switch from deep pools of curiosity to "Don't fuck with me."

Grub would appear for weeks at a time and disappear as suddenly as he came.

Grub helped Dad junk cars and resell them as recycled scrap metal, which entailed stripping the cars of parts we could sell and then crushing the car frame—complete with seats, glass, engines, and transmissions—into a metal pancake.

Dad invented a monster portable car crusher. Based on plans he scribbled on a piece of paper he kept folded in his wallet, Dad built this fantastic machine himself, welding second-hand nuclear submarine parts and hydraulic pistons to various heavy steel odds and ends he secured from nearby military salvage auctions. Once finished, the thing towered over us at 20 feet high. It looked like it belonged on a B-rated science fiction movie set.

For years, the dynamic car-crushing duo of Grub and Dad would use our dilapidated payloader to stack the crushed car carcasses in piles on the back of an eighteen-wheeler. Once the flatbed was filled and the cab packed with the necessities—a few cartons of cigs and a thermos of coffee—they disappeared up north to the Promised Land of Canadian steel mills. They left, hearts happy and hopeful they would return with full pockets as long as the price per ton for recycled steel was high and they didn't get swindled out of it on the way home or take a detour to the race track.

Another "gent" around the table was the colorful Pressie, all 300 pounds of him. I never knew his first name, but I did know that my brother told me that after drinking several whiskey shots at my sister Cindy's wedding reception, he took a domestic dispute to new heights when he pointed a gun at his wife. Two brave guys wrestled him to the ground and grabbed his gun away. My brother Ryan was assigned to take him home to sleep it off. I can't imagine how Ryan got him in and out of the car, but I know that it took months to get the smell of Pressie's vomit out of his car upholstery.

You didn't cross Pressie. It was rumored he had ties to the Mafia. That may have been true because he treated Dad like *famiglia,* complete with unquestioned loyalty. It suddenly appeared when Dad needed anything—money, a piece of expensive heavy equipment for the yard, or a new household appliance—no questions asked.

Charlie and Seb were probably the worst of the lot. They became a team when they worked for the circus "taking care" of the elephants. In reality, they beat the poor animals to get them to do what they wanted. Dad even warned me to stay away from them. They must have been bad news because I don't remember him warning me about anyone else. Dad said Charlie had been thrown out of Mexico as "an undesirable."

These two pals joined the circus in Florida and worked their way up the Eastern shore until they reached Connecticut. They then quit and came to live with us for a bit, building a makeshift apartment out of a few connected cars down in the yard.

They used a crowbar to take off wheel rims to raise some cash. Dad offered a quarter per rim—stacking them not too far from our house so any customer who needed one could easily find the right size and buy it for a few bucks. When Seb and Charlie had enough money for a fifth of vodka, they quit for the day and were good for the night.

When they didn't feel like popping wheel rims, they visited local campgrounds and found tents whose occupants were not there—most likely taking in local hiking trails or swimming holes—and wiped the campsite clean. Those bastards took everything—sometimes including the tent—and sold it out of the back of their truck farther down the road.

On one particular visit, Seb caught the "entrepreneurial spirit," according to my dad, and got into the Christmas tree business. Dad said Seb needed to lay low due to some "problems" in Florida, so he stayed up north with us that winter. I didn't even think about where he got the trees, but later learned he'd cut them down on land he didn't own—even stealing some from the front lawns of sleeping homeowners. He'd pull off the side of a rural road and sell the trees to unsuspecting holiday shoppers. I always thought it was pretty ingenious. Having read a few detective novels, I realized there were no serial numbers to trace on a stolen pine tree. Brilliant!

Eventually, the circus would return—and they'd team up again to head south for the winter.

Mr. Payne, we called him Mr. P for various reasons, sat around the table for longer than anyone else, yet he is the one I have the most difficulty describing. Short and somewhat muscular, he had sandy brown hair, his bangs often hanging in his small sunken eyes; leathery skin that had seen too much sun; and sported cut-off shorts way too short for any man to wear.

When I asked how he came to live with us, I was told that Mr. P arrived because he needed a part for his truck and never left. I guess he couldn't pay for it, so my dad offered—as he had to many others in similar situations—that he could stay and work in the yard to pay it off.

He stayed for years. I don't recall a time when he wasn't there. He helped Dad in the yard, doing whatever was needed.

He started living in his car and eventually moved into the house, living in the room upstairs just across the hall from us kids' bedrooms.

He had a small TV on his bedside dresser that he'd let us watch whatever we wanted. We'd have to sit on his bed with him to see the TV, but we didn't mind. He gave us rides in his truck—often going for ice cream. He watched us, and I mistook that for watching out for us.

He was also a friend. Constant. Someone we could rely on for a ride to school if we missed the bus or extra cash for something we felt we couldn't ask Mom or Dad for.

Mr. P was broken and, in turn, broke many of us. He broke me.

It was complicated.

Despite the shifty characters my parents exposed us to, I have no idea if Mom and Dad ever felt we were in danger. However, I can't imagine that if they did, they wouldn't have done anything about it. I do not know how they could have known about Mr. P and what he did at night upstairs above their sleeping heads—and not stop it.

Growing up with unpredictability, I learned to be ready to react. I'd cope by getting lost in pretending when something happened unexpectedly or was scary. Pretending was my superpower. When the current reality hurt, I'd create a new scenario—an alternative reality I could live with.

Jagged Shards of Memory

I'M SLIGHTLY ANNOYED AND BLINDED BY THE LIGHT SHINING FROM THE BATHROOM as I wait for Rich, my husband of thirty-three years, to finish at the sink and come to bed. Then it happens. Glancing out of the corner of my eye, I notice his backlit male body silhouetted in the doorway. My brain doesn't skip a beat as my retina registers the image, and I immediately gasp and hold my breath as adrenaline and fear grip my body.

In milliseconds, I'm no longer a wife waiting for the man she loves to crawl into bed but a child in my bedroom on the second floor of our house in the junkyard. I'm gripping the sheets with my fingers, simultaneously squeezing my eyes shut as I hope this will trick him into thinking I'm asleep.

Holding my breath, I peek my eyes open to see him watching me from the doorway with that sickening grin. I see him, his tight-fitting cut-off jean shorts backlit by the hallway light, tugging at a pulsating bulge beneath the front zipper. I close my eyes, the darkness accentuating the sound of his heavy but quickening breath and a slow, low groan coming from his throat. I hope he'll return to his bed across the hall after he's finished. Praying that will be enough for him tonight.

Mr. P was one of the strangers around the table who never left. Honestly, I don't remember a time when he wasn't there. I feel weird admitting this, but he's even in my wedding album—several photos of him standing alongside the bride and groom, smiling for the camera. But that's another story.

Years later, my older brother Ryan reminded me that Mr. P made himself indispensable, so my parents let him move into our house. Later my little brother moved into his room across the hall from Maddy and mine.

When Mr. P first moved in, we kids thought it was cool because he brought a little TV with him. It sat on the beat-up bureau that separated my little brother Jack's twin bed from Mr. P's. We'd never heard of having a TV next to your bed!

Mr. P would let us watch whatever we wanted. I recall watching episodes of *Petticoat Junction*, *Bewitched*, and *Gilligan's Island* as we lay on the bed with him. Occasionally, I fantasized about being as beautiful as Ginger, as inventive as Gilligan, and as smart as the Professor.

I distinctly remember watching Elizabeth Montgomery in *Bewitched* use her magic to get herself out of a jam, running to my room and doing my best imitation of her. I'd twitch and wiggle my nose as hard as I could, wishing I could be somewhere else or that Mr. P would go away (but leave his TV).

When that didn't happen, I figured maybe my wish was too big, so I tried for something "smaller," such as instantly cleaning my room. When that didn't work, I watched the episodes carefully the next week, taking notes in my Barbie spiral notebook, hoping Samantha might reveal the secret to making it work. But no such luck.

My memories around Mr. P get confusing and fuzzy–like a never-ending bad dream sequence with time lapses and events that don't make sense. These memories are sharp fragments like shards of a mirror with jagged edges. No matter how I piece them together, the reflection is distorted, never able to reflect the truth.

After many years—and various therapists—I've come to believe that my flawed memory is good. Thankfully, my brain's built-in protection mechanism has been selectively hiding some of my most painful childhood memories.

This is why—even to this day—I question if I'm making some of this up. But why would I make this shit up?

Mr. P was a clever monster.

He had a cool pickup truck that he'd use to take us kids out for ice cream and for rides to cool off on hot summer nights. I remember feeling so free and happy sitting in the back of the pickup, my hair whipping around my face in the rush of the wind, laughing so hard with my sister and brother as we gripped the sides of the truck's bed so we wouldn't fall out. As we sped down the road, I felt brave and invincible.

I was brave and invincible.

Mr. P and I had a "special relationship" for years. It changed occasionally, and I was too little to understand that it wasn't okay. He varied what we'd do so much that I never knew what to expect. It was like being on high alert all the time. Sometimes he'd just want to watch me or have me watch him; other times, he'd have me touch him, or he'd touch me. It was a game I always lost.

I've been asked whether I remember specifics. I do, but I question if what I recall actually happened. Most of what I can remember are shards of sensory memories that I try to piece together: rubbing sensations that hurt, a warm sticky substance that tasted salty; my lips raw and chapped; my jaw—and other body parts—sore for days. I felt sharp pain mixed with an odd sense of relief—or was it release or pleasure? I can't be sure.

I am not clear on when our "special relationship" started or ended. It's all a blur. Could it have begun as early as age five or six? Perhaps it stopped when I got my period at age thirteen. I think I was too old, or it had become too risky. My therapists believed I was no longer his "type."

Even as a child, I knew my life would drastically change if I told anyone—especially my father—and not for the better. I knew my father's temper and imagined he'd grab that gun in the back of his bedroom closet, point it at Mr. P, and end it. It would also be the end of our family.

So I made deals with the devil.

If I missed a bus and was afraid to tell my parents, I'd wake Mr. P, and he'd take me, both of us knowing I'd pay him back later. If I wanted something new to wear to a party, he'd give me some cash to help me buy it, along with an unspoken IOU. If I needed to just get in that pickup truck and let my hair blow in the wind to forget about life, he'd understand and take me for that ride and another later.

My childhood brain laser-focused on what he gave me. My adult brain became only too aware of what he had taken away.

My innocence.

My virginity when I didn't even know what it was.

The ability for me to have friends over for sleepovers. (I knew I had to protect others from him.)

And I'm aware of one thing he took away almost every day.

He denied me the unabashed pleasure of physical desire for the man I love more than anything. He took away my ability to let my body respond in a natural, passionate way to physical touch and intimacy. He makes me push my husband away and say, "No, not tonight," more often than I allow myself to melt into his loving embrace.

I sometimes feel that what Mr. P left is an empty shell of a woman.

I have spent years in various forms of therapy to unravel all the stories I made up to protect myself, dig deep to retrieve memories, and make sense of them. I'm working hard to rewire my brain and my body. Despite doing this deep healing work, even today, as I write my story, I still feel like I am making it all up.

After sixty years, when my husband's silhouette still has the power to trigger me, it confirms how real it was. My body and my brain cannot lie.

Don't Cross the Line

IF CHICKS ARE COMPLICATED, THEN SISTERS CAN BE COMBUSTIBLE.

"Stay on your side of the room," Maddy sniped. "And don't mess up my side. I just cleaned it up." Gingerly stepping across "her side" of the brown worn shag carpet, I safely made it to my side of our bedroom, next to the closet door.

Our lopsided twin beds sag toward two windows overlooking piles of tires, a worn swing set, and a corrugated metal office building. The sun shone through the dirty windows on that day, casting beams across the room. Plopping on my bed, I saw tiny dust particles floating in the air. Noting that my hanging plants needed water, I took pride in the natural jute macramé plant holders I'd made, completing another Girl Scout badge.

I don't remember what color bedspread I was lying on—or even if we had ones that matched—but stretching out on that twin bed felt like a brand-new Sealy Posturepedic because it was all mine. When we were little, the three of us—Jack, Maddy, and I—shared one bed. As Maddy and I became young women, Mom and Dad realized Jack shouldn't be sharing a bed with us, so they moved Jack into Mr. P's room across the hall.

Leaning back—my pillow resting against my Bobbie Sherman tribute wall, plastered with photos I had cut out of *Teen Beat* magazine—I tried to relax but couldn't.

Maddy was in a bad mood. And so was I.

I sighed, slumping further down the wall, heavy from the pain of not having a small white envelope with my name on it in my book bag—an invite to a fourteenth birthday party. Kim needed to be more discreet in handing out the envelopes to everyone at the lunch table. To everyone, that is, except me. At least Robin had tried to hide hers by sliding it immediately into her lunch box as she gave me a little smile and a shrug from across the table. Robin was my best friend, but she had many other best friends and was often included on invite lists that I wasn't. It had happened before and would happen again.

I sank further into my bed, my disappointment and anger swelling as I quickly found a target. Across from me sat my little sister Maddy. I looked at her strong gymnast's body, muscles showing beneath the gymnastics getup, her rosy heart-shaped face framed by perfectly feathered blonde hair. Why did she have to be so pretty and athletic?

Years later, when we were both in high school, a totally out-of-my-league guy approached my locker, and asked for my phone number. While he wrote the phone number on the back of his notebook, he quickly asked, crushing my hopes in an instant, "You're Maddy's sister, right?" No sooner had I muttered a yes than he quickly scribbled her name next to the number and walked away.

Maddy and I found our own tribes in high school. Maddy was on varsity sports teams, the honor society, popular socially, spontaneous, and comfortable in her own skin. I had a tight social circle of friends, was captain of cheerleading, on the student council, and a dramatic theater geek who could only let loose when I was on stage being someone else.

Maddy and I fought a lot. Big brawls. Maddy with fists; me with words.

After sitting awhile on our beds, my eyes settled on my prize possession—a genuine GE plastic portable record player with built-in stereophonic sound speakers. The red-and-white turntable rested on a stool under the window, and I noticed that the stylus arm wasn't in its place. My eyes darted to the stack of records on the floor. My new Elton John album, purchased with hard-earned babysitting money, wasn't appropriately stored in the album sleeve. Maddy had been playing my records.

Her eyes followed mine, realizing I was figuring out her transgression. Maddy's fists clenched in the exact instant my mind raced to think of the most hurtful things to say.

Before we knew it—the insults and punches were flying. Unaware of how long we fought, we stopped short when Dad appeared in the doorway.

We had awakened him. He wasn't happy. Dad's sleep schedule, often staying up late into the night, reading or talking with the guys, meant it wasn't unusual for him to be in bed when we got home from our after-school activities. He'd joke about the fact he slept when other dads weren't. Rather than admit he was taking a much-needed nap, he said was "resting his clothes"—they just happened to be on him!

"Goddamn it, you two! Shut the fuck up!" he shouted as he walked into our room, his greasy hair sticking straight up. He raised his arms over his head, revealing the underarm stains on his dirty white T-shirt. "Learn to live together, goddamn it."

I interrupted him, blurting out how she kept getting into my stuff as Maddy whined how sick and tired she was of having my stuff all over the room. We were both shouting and talking so fast we didn't notice he'd left in a huff.

Before we knew it, he was back with a can of spray paint. Without hesitation, Dad sprayed a black line down the wall between the windows and right across the carpet between the twin beds.

Mouths open and momentarily speechless, we just stood near the doorway.

Dad grabbed me by the arm and jerked me toward my bed. "This side is yours—keep your fucking stuff on it," he said. Shoving Maddy hard enough that she fell backward on her bed, he added, "And you, Maddy, this is your side. Don't use anything that's across that line, you hear?"

Gaining my senses and an ounce of courage, I sat up and felt the need to point out that Maddy had the doorway on her side. "How am I supposed to get in and out of my side?" I asked with a defiant tone.

"Okay, smartass," Dad said, pointing to a small swath of carpet that led from the hallway to my side of the room. Thankfully, he didn't start painting again. "That there is neutral territory. Got it?"

Dad turned and left. Maddy and I looked at each other, breathing in the fumes of the paint particle mist still settling in the air and watching a not-so-straight line of paint drip down the wall.

That line between Maddy and me was there for decades.

I suspect Mr. P had something to do with keeping the line there. I imagine fear and keeping silent about what was happening with Mr. P strengthened the line. The line somehow prevented Maddy from knowing what was happening on my side and me from knowing what was happening on hers. Somehow, I felt that this line—this separation—could protect her too.

Years later, Maddy told me she remembered sitting with her back to our bedroom door, her feet up for extra leverage against our dresser to keep Mr. P out. I never knew she did that. I never knew she knew. Perhaps we could have talked about it sooner if the line hadn't existed. We could have supported each other.

Short Shorts

THE SUN WARMED MY BARE BACK, WHICH WAS EXPOSED BY MY HOMEMADE HALTER top comprising two red bandanas twisted and turned every which way to conceal my budding thirteen-year-old breasts. I crossed the blacktop road off Route 81, glancing to the right and left to ensure it was safe to cross.

It was one of the hottest July days of that summer. I was on my way home from our closest neighbors, the Planskys. Lately, Kat, Terry, and I had been hanging out in their backyard. Mrs. Plansky always had a whole pitcher of Kool-Aid—our favorite being Blasting Berry Cherry or Mountainberry Punch. We'd sip from our Dixie cups under the shade of a tree in their backyard. There was very little shade at our house. Plus, there was nowhere to hide from the eyes of customers.

Today, we munched on Mrs. Plansky's peanut butter and fluff sandwiches on Wonder bread as we straddled the legs of our mismatched aluminum webbed chairs over the sides of a kiddie pool.

A few years earlier, we were caught swimming in a " pond" that suddenly appeared in their backyard, only to find it was their sewer overflowing. Mom and Dad could smell us before we even entered the house.

This time, our feet were cool as they dangled in the clear, clean water in the kiddie pool. We talked and lazily flipped the worn pages of old magazines, most likely nicked from the hair salon in town. We were determined to find the right hairstyle that might make us look more sophisticated as we anticipated our entry into Haddam Killingworth High School in September.

It was a short walk back home, but I had to cross and walk along a busy section of Route 81 until I reached the overgrown lower entrance to the junkyard. This entrance had been closed several years ago when Dad had the guys install an abandoned piece of rusted chain-link fence. The objective was to make it nearly impossible for anyone to sneak into the junkyard and steal car parts from Dad.

Before installing the fence, at least once or twice a month, the junkyard dogs dad kept outside to guard the yard, would bark in the middle of the night, and Dad would go outside in his sagging Fruit of the Loom underwear, 22 in his hand. He'd point the gun and shoot up into the sky, signaling warning shots to anyone who had snuck in to steal his property. Often, the police would arrive shortly afterward in response to a neighbor calling in what they had heard. Dad, friendly with most of the local guys in blue, would often invite them in for a cup of coffee.

While Dad felt secure that the fence kept out most of the riffraff, I had discovered a thin break in the wall that I could cut through on my walk home from school or the Planskys. From there, I would follow the dusty path past my grandparents' house and through the junkyard to make my way up the hill to our house.

Walking so exposed on Route 81 always made me a bit paranoid as my inner radar would automatically kick into high alert. I would nervously walk faster and faster, picking up the pace purposefully until I could relax a bit once I was safely behind the chain-link fence. Until I reached the safety of the lower junkyard, my eyes would dart ahead to how far I had to go and back to the road to see who was approaching me from each direction. It was a busy road, and you just never knew who might be zip by or slow down.

Sometimes I'd make a game of trying to read and memorize the license plates as they whizzed by. This task helped me calm my mind. Other times, I'd ride my bike, feeling safer because I pedaled faster than I would walk.

Today, I walked and tugged at the nonexistent legs of my shorts, only now being quite conscious of how short they were. I realized they were getting even shorter as they rode higher and higher with each step I took. I had been proud of my shorts just a few hours earlier, having bragged to Kat and Terry about how I had cut them from an old pair of jeans this morning. I had neglected to share how I ended up snipping the legs shorter and shorter to make the two sides even. The result was reminiscent of the many times Mom cut our bangs too short after too many attempts to make them even. Once it was cut, there was no turning back. Tugging at my shorts, I remembered awkward school photos to prove the last-minute "trims" mom performed before picture day. I should have stopped trying to make them perfect.

Realizing I'd have to ditch the shorts as soon as I got home before Dad or Mom saw them, my thoughts were interrupted by the loud shrill of multiple whistles emerging from the open windows of a rusted-out pickup truck that was passing by. When I looked up, I saw it slow down and pull over just ahead, right in front of the old driveway, blocking my worn path to safety behind the fence.

My heart started pumping so fast and hard that I thought it would leap out of my chest. I felt a jolt of adrenaline as fear gripped me. Someone opened the cab's front passenger-side door, and I froze about ten feet from the truck. Before I knew it, a man stood before me, blocking my path to the driveway. He was laughing at something someone in the cab had said, and I noticed he tugged at his pants, making an "adjustment" near his zipper. My eyes, anxious to move away from what I saw, glanced up toward his face only to register an oddly familiar grin showing yellowing teeth. Instantly, I felt a shock run through me. "Where you headed, pretty little lady?" he asked. "Why don't you hop on in, and we'll give you a ride?"

Someone inside drawled, "Yeahhhhhh, I'll give you a ride, sweet thing." More laughter.

Alarm bells rang inside, and before I knew it, my legs took a sharp right-hand turn and led me directly into the woods. I felt the sting of branches snapping back and hitting my face and legs, cutting me as I ran as fast as possible. I was moving forward blindly, not daring to waste a second to look back to know if I was being followed. I kept cutting through the wooded lot, stumbling, eventually making it to the dirt path that wove through the lower junkyard. I didn't slow down until I was up the hill and inside our house.

Out of breath, I stood still inside our door, panting. It was only then that I felt safe and started to cry.

I looked up and saw Mom, startled, sitting at the kitchen table, a cigarette stub smoking beside her in the ashtray, hands folded around the stained coffee mug. "What the hell?" she said. "What is wrong, Laurie?"

I was wheezing and coughing and crying. I noticed the scrapes and scratches on my legs and arms. I was a total sweaty, bloody mess. My long hair stuck to my face as my heart beat fast and furious from the combined physical exertion of the sprint and the alarm of the situation I had just experienced. I tried to say something in response, but all that came out were gasps for breath as I almost fell to the floor.

"What in god's name happened," Mom said, moving her chair to fully inspect me.

"Mom, there was this truck. A guy came out and tried to take me. Mom, he was going to—" I stammered and sobbed.

"Are you sure? Nonsense, Laurie. Tell me what actually happened," she demanded.

I slowly caught my breath and explained what had happened and how I had narrowly escaped what I was sure to have been a horrific fate. Mom interrupted me with a sigh and sat back in her chair.

Reaching for her cigarette she continued, "Laurie, why do you have to be so dramatic? I'm sure those guys were going to ask you for directions or something. Maybe they just wanted to see if you needed a ride home. Really, not everyone is out to get you, you know. For heaven's sake. You're just a kid."

She looked at me, and I knew she didn't believe me. She'd never believe me. She thought I had made this up.

"Calm down, go upstairs, and clean yourself up. You are okay. We'll eat soon; I don't want to hear another word about this. You're making stuff up again."

Still shaking, I went to the bathroom and cleaned up my legs and arms. I stood at the sink and ran some warm water into the basin. I wet a ragged washcloth and started to wipe away the grime and shame. Wiping myself harder and harder, the hurt I felt transferred to my skin appearing in random red and rough blotches. I was rubbing with all my anger and hurt.

I dragged my red and irritated body upstairs. I was cleaner and calmer. I sat on my bed, picked up my latest Nancy Drew, and got lost in her mystery for a bit. My breath returned to its regular cadence. I thought about what Mom had said. She had called me a drama queen before, and I sometimes made stuff up. She was right about that. I had embellished things in the past. But this did happen. I had been in danger. That was real. *Wasn't it?*

As my nervous system calmed down, the details of the drama began to fade and soften.

I looked down at the short shorts I still had on. Anger arose, and I tugged them off and threw them in the trash, confident they were to blame. As I put on a pair of regular-length shorts, I was thankful Mom hadn't noticed how short my short shorts were when I came in. She must have been preoccupied.

I went downstairs to watch TV. *Dark Shadows* would be on.

Queen of Domesticity

THIS WAS IT. SEVENTH GRADE. THE BIG TIME.

As I dressed that morning, I was nervous and excited. Would I find my locker? What if I couldn't find homeroom or the locations of all my classes? As I pulled on the brightly colored, crocheted, granny-square vest Mom had made for me over my long-sleeved t-shirt, I wondered who might have a locker next to mine. I strained to remember who else had a last name that might be listed on the seventh-grade Haddam Killingworth High School roster before or after the name Watson. Then, my heart skipped a beat. *Is it possible that my best friend Robin Walsh's locker may not be that far from mine?* I relaxed and felt a bit more confident, smiling inside in anticipation.

All that confidence faded as I entered the crowded hallway overflowing with seventh- through twelfth-grade students. I felt invisible as I was jostled and bumped by others running to greet friends or make their way to their lockers. My less-than-five-foot frame was dwarfed, and I felt suffocated as what seemed like the entire high school basketball team loomed above me, circling and speeding past. A tide of teenagers almost took me away as I attempted to find the outer edges of the hallway to read the locker numbers so I could locate mine. Suddenly, I was jerked toward the wall by some unforeseen force. The familiar sweet scent of Love's Baby Soft body splash hit my nose, instantly calming me.

It was Robin to the rescue. "Hey, have you found your locker yet?" she questioned as I noticed her outfit, straight out of the JCPenney catalog. *Was that the tent dress with the awesome collar we had both circled and admired over the summer when planning the perfect wardrobe we'd buy if our parents had suddenly won the lottery? Wait! Was Robin wearing a bra underneath?*

I was about to ask her when she jerked me further down the hallway. We were high school salmon swimming upstream for the first time.

My sister Cindy had given me some tips for navigating high school. She told me I'd have to try harder to fit in if I wanted people to like me. She suggested I get cooler clothes—maybe have Mom hem some of my skirts shorter and urged me to do something different with my hair. I had been proud of my long hair and didn't think I'd have any problem fitting in, but now that I was here, I was beginning to understand. I looked like Wednesday from the Addams family, a thin line of my white scalp—like an exclamation mark—running right down the middle of my head, dramatically parting my mousy dark hair.

I began to notice others around me for comparison. *Who are these people? Where do they come from? Did something magical happen in the summer of 1974 that made everyone except me taller, prettier, and cooler?*

It was as if a veil had lifted, and all I saw were the "cool" people. Guys with flowing golden curls, their muscles bursting out of their short-sleeve T-shirts as they leaned over their perfect girlfriends' white smiles surrounded by glossy lips leaning voluptuously at their lockers. *Who were these beautiful gods and goddesses?*

Hours later, I was sitting in Home Ec 101, the class I had dreamed about taking all summer. I took in the gleaming surroundings of a classroom like none I'd ever experienced before. To the right were several mini-kitchens with genuine GE electric stoves, Whirlpool refrigerators, and Formica counters bleach-clean and teamed with new-looking kitchen gadgets lined up in a neat row. On the opposite wall were sewing stations sporting Singer sewing machines perched on top like shiny symbols of domesticity.

What promise that classroom held.

Boy, was I wrong.

Months later, sitting in front of one of those sewing stations, I stood gleefully anticipating our prim and proper teacher, wearing the bright white apron with her name embroidered, handing out our final grades for our sewing unit. My mom was a super seamstress, and feeling this talent must be genetic, I was confident my flannel nightgown would garner an A.

I remember how proud Mom was when she brought me to her favorite fabric store a month earlier and let me purchase the bright pink flannel with pastel puppies and kittens printed on it that wasn't on the clearance rack. I couldn't wait to bring my project home to show her.

All thoughts of a mother-daughter moment of domestic bliss vanished as Mrs. Drew handed me my project. She noted, "Now, class, attention to details of the pattern instructions is paramount in sewing," looking at me with a knowing smile. "We can get ahead of ourselves and keep sewing without being aware of the symbols on the paper pattern."

I looked at my nightgown. She had marked a C on the checklist. A C! I don't think I had ever gotten anything below a B—ever. A handwritten note on the bottom said, "Great seams and effort, Laurie, but I'm not sure how you anticipate wearing this. Check out your bottom hem."

I looked at the bottom of the nightgown. I sunk into my chair, hoping no one else noticed. I had sewed up the bottom as if it were a sleeping bag. There was no way to put the nightgown on.

I was mortified.

Later that night, I nervously pulled my project out of my backpack to show Mom what I had done. Smiling, Mom handed me a seam ripper and said, "You did a nice even, straight stitch—but it has to go. You'll get the hang of it."

While that was the beginning and end of my sewing career, that lesson and the warmth of Mom's confidence in me began something. It stirred up something inside that would grow.

I had spent so much time and effort to make the details perfect—sewing as close as I could to the lines of the pattern, being oh so careful not to veer too far off of center—that I had neglected to step back and take in the bigger picture of the entire pattern.

This was more than just missing a critical instruction and making a mistake. This indicated the lessons that would be there for me not just in my high school years—but for my life.

I would desperately seek my ballast amongst the storm during those school years, riding those tumultuous hormone-fueled teenaged emotional waves—often in a state of confusion. I had to find my center—my identity. I was inventing myself while at the same time trying to see who I really was underneath all the stuff that had happened to me, independent of being a junkyard girl. The only way I knew how to do that was to get lost in the effort to be anyone I thought the world wanted me to be. Someone acceptable.

I couldn't hide. Things I did that were "wrong" would be found out. I knew I'd survive because I already had. I was beginning to work out just how I might fit into this world, what my life could mean, and what it—and I—could become.

This unfurling of self like a frond unfolding to its fern potential would indeed grow—be it in fits and starts. I would slowly recognize my center even while fighting and finding my way upstream. I'd not only ride those emotional waves—I'd surf them like a master. Eventually.

PART THREE

The Power of Pretend

If You Don't Like My Peaches

IT WAS HALLOWEEN. MOM'S FAVORITE HOLIDAY. SHE LOVED TO CREATE OUR costumes but also to take on a new persona herself.

This particular Halloween, Mom's hair was teased and piled up, making her head look lopsided, with a ball of matted hair on the right side of her face. She looked rough and was wearing one of Dad's ratty flannel shirts with a pillow stuffed in it, so she appeared to have a giant beer belly.

Her face lit up as if she remembered something she had forgotten. She smiled, revealing that she had used licorice gum to blacken a few teeth. She ran into her bedroom, and I could hear her rummaging through the pile of things on the worn dresser with the missing top drawer. Walking out of her bedroom, she was pinning a large circular button on her shirt. It said, "If you don't like my peaches, don't shake my tree." Her Halloween outfit was complete.

When I think back to that button, it fit Mom perfectly. She was a woman to reckon with. You didn't mess with Mom once she had her mind set on something. I'm not sure where she inherited this from. Grandma Josephine seemed much more subdued, but perhaps her edge had softened in her later years.

Never letting things slide—Mom did not hesitate to march right into the principal's office without an appointment when some kids stole my glasses on the bus and broke them—then tormented me when I had to wear them with white first aid tape holding them in place at the bridge.

Mom worked tirelessly to make us clothes that looked just as fashionable as those you could get at JCPenney, driving an hour to a discounted fabric place to find just the right look for the project at hand that fit her budget. She was the right amount of sneaky when she squirreled away crumpled fives and ones in a box in the recesses of her dresser so we'd have extra cash for things Dad deemed unnecessary. It was always our secret when she went to her private bank to make a withdrawal.

Mom was also a lot of fun.

That Halloween, after Mom donned that pin, she was on task. Our costumes were most likely homemade and fabulous. Whatever we dreamed up—Mom created. I remember winning multiple church costume contests. Once, she made me a black-and-white furry Pepé Le Pew costume. She even gave me one of those perfume bottles with the ball you could squeeze so I could spritz people with perfume. One year, Maddy wanted to be a haystack. Mom dressed her in tan turtleneck and slacks and roped real hay around her. (No one invited her into their home that year for fear she'd leave a trail of hay!) Jack liked store-bought costumes. He liked his face being completely covered by a plastic mask.

Mom loved Halloween more than we did. She liked to pretend, too.

She enjoyed the surprised look on her friends' faces when she showed up as something unexpected. For some years, she kept it simple. Dressing up like a bum or homeless person. One year, she was Phyllis Diller, but I don't know if anyone immediately guessed who she was. You'd think the long cigarette holder and her hair teased up and spiked and stiff in every direction—thanks to a generous application of Aqua Net—would have given it away. We all thought it was great and told her so!

Route 81 was a busy road, so every Halloween, Mom drove us to some of her friends' houses and a few of the neighbors' houses, several of whom were part of the Plansky family—their kids were partners in crime with us for many adventures.

By the night's end, we'd end up at the Saint James Church Hall, where the Stokes—an older couple from church—held a little party every Halloween for families from the congregation. We loved that stop. I especially looked forward to showing Mrs. Stokes my costume. She would sneak full-sized candy bars into my bag. She also had homemade treats and fun games.

Mom would brush off the compliments of how clever her costume was as if she had pulled it together at a moment's notice when she had worked on it for most of the week. I'd see her laughing, and she seemed lighter, enjoying the company of other adults talking about ordinary things while we kids gathered around the games. Since that was our last stop, we didn't mind ruining our Halloween makeup or costumes.

We'd kneel to bob for apples in a tin washtub set up over a plastic tablecloth on the floor or struggle to bite them as they hung suspended from the ceiling by a string. Jostling to get in with who we thought would be the "winning team," we'd have ants in our pants waiting for our turn to carry raw eggs in a spoon over the masking taped finish line across the room.

One year, they organized a burlap sack race. But once we got in the sacks, it was a free-for-all as we hopped into each other, falling down laughing and creating more of a burlap-sack bumper-car experience.

Thinking of the kindness of church members putting on such a fabulous Halloween party, I can't help but remember Mrs. Schmidt, who lived across the street. Some afternoons, she'd yell, "Woo-hoo! Kids!" from across the road after the school bus dropped us off. "Come on in for a bit." We always went because we knew what that meant. Giant-sized chocolate chip cookies—larger than a teacup saucer and thin, crisp, and warm from the oven—would be waiting for us in her cheery kitchen. She had one of those ancient big black stoves, similar to one Grandma Watson had but bigger. I don't remember if she baked those cookies in it, but I didn't care where they came from. We'd gobble them with cold milk served in Welch's Flintstones jelly glasses. I always wanted Pebbles or Bamm-Bamm, and it felt like a good day if I got one.

Eventually, we'd finally make it down the hill to the house, our chocolate-smeared smiles indicating to Mom where we had been.

More Than Words

BOOKS WERE ONE OF MY SAFE PLACES, DULLING PAINFUL MOMENTS AND TAKING
me far away from the realities of living in a junkyard.

When I close my eyes, I can picture the tall concrete columns support-ing our small town library's majestic roof protecting its brick facade. The entrance door, flanked by several tall pillars, could have been intimi-dating to others but was inviting to me. It was as if the library held a strength that I needed. I believe it was that strength that lured me inside.

I can still transport myself there. Upon crossing the vestibule, I'd take a deep breath and exhale all of my worries. The familiar musty smell of damp books—many that hadn't been moved, or read for that matter, for years—would mingle with the sweet scent of Jean Nate from the older librarian behind the checkout desk.

I would relax.

Standing on tippy-toes to see inside the wooden card catalog, I remember how hard it was to pull the drawers. They often got stuck on the rails and required a strong tug, risking that the entire heavy drawer would suddenly thrust out and spill all of those carefully ordered cards.

Thanks to my mom's love of reading—and the fact that there was ample heat in the winter and damp, cool air noisily blowing from ancient air conditioning units in the summer—our family were regular patrons of Brainerd Memorial Library for as long as I can remember. While I don't have a clear picture of the librarian's face, I remember her soft, animated voice as we sat cross-legged on dirty carpet squares, eagerly listening during weekly storytime.

Sitting up straight, knees and feet tucked underneath me so I could gain a bit extra height to see the pictures she held up, I'd often limp away from story time in pain, legs numb with pins and needles but happy. It was worth the pain to be transported to another place and time.

Mom left during story hour, escaping to the periodical section to catch up on the latest *Good Housekeeping* or *Life* magazine, ensuring she had time to check out another juicy Sidney Sheldon novel. Years later, Mom would often drop me off, and I'd spend an entire day traveling through time with my nose in a book. If Mom was too busy to take me, I'd cajole someone—Cindy or Mr. P—for a lift. On the rare occasion they couldn't, I'd resort to riding my bike the 4 miles down busy Route 81 through downtown Higganum and struggle up the hill to arrive at my literacy sanctuary to get my story fix. Most of the time, I needed help to zip up my bulging bookbag with my borrowed treasures before cycling home.

As a teen, I'd find an unoccupied aisle, quietly select a book from the shelf, and slide down to the floor until I was nestled between the stacks. I would be so absorbed in the story that hours later, at closing time, I would have gotten locked inside if the librarian hadn't flicked the lights on and off—knowing I was still there—patiently waiting for me as I scrambled toward the door, yelling from the darkness "I'm coming!"

My love affair with libraries continued into college.

At Marist College, I had the perfect job. I worked for Jim, our campus postmaster. Because I sorted and delivered mail, I knew which guys were two-timing as they would come to pick up their mail arm in arm with their Marist girlfriends and quickly stash the scented envelopes they got from their girl back home (decorated with Xs, Os, and hearts) in their pockets. Jim would look the other way and pretend he didn't see us as we flipped through *Vogue* and *Woman's Wear Daily* magazines during our break before putting them into the correct mailboxes. After mail delivery, if I was manning the window—I usually had plenty of time to do homework, and he often let me come in later if I had early morning crew practice at dawn.

While I had always been up early at home, this was different. Back then, early mornings were a necessity—chaotic and rushed. At Marist, I chose to rise early, and it was pure joy. I loved the serenity of mornings in the Hudson Valley. When I had crew practice on the Hudson River at dawn, I saw and felt the cool mist floating up off the river. Walking back to the dorm after practice, I felt calmed by the sounds of silence before they were interrupted inside the dorm by my fellow co-eds waking to their clock radio alarms blaring Grateful Dead or Marshall Tucker Band. If I didn't have crew or work, I'd be at the library just as the massive doors were being unlocked.

I loved that library. The openness of it. The knowledge within. It became my safe place on campus. I'd pick my favorite spot early for the day, often camping out there for hours and hours.

My love of reading—and later my flair for any form of theatrics—opened up many possibilities. I found comfort in books and any type of performance.

Singing alto in the chorus in high school, I loved my voice harmonizing with those surrounding me. When I sang, I was somewhere else. It wasn't long before my music teacher recruited me to try out for the school musicals. Acting permitted me to become someone else others could see. A person I could be proud to be. It allowed me to not just "try on someone else's shoes," as my dad would say, but their entire life.

I loved being someone else so much that I almost majored in drama and theater in college but later settled on writing and communications, thinking there were more opportunities for real jobs with more money.

But my love affair with any form of storytelling would stay with me. Stories taught me about the world. Stories are how I can share a slice of my life with others so they can be right there with me. I love how weaving the details of a good story allows us to be transported in time and place.

There is magic in digging deep inside and owning our story—dissecting it scene by scene, offering true insight and a better understanding of our emotions, behaviors, and reactions to whatever life throws at us. I know that when I've done this, healing takes center stage. The more vulnerable I am, the more I uncover my truth. Words said and written feel like the truth.

Yet, it is hard to separate fact from fiction with a childhood like mine. What is the truth when my memories are a mashup of what happened in my life and what I wished had happened? How can I discount stories I made up that saved me, offering me a way out?

When my memories and the stories I recall from back then feel like my truth, aren't they my truth?

Solid as a Rock

MY REFUGE WAS A ROCK IN THE WOODS THAT JUTTED INTO THE CREEK. IT WAS probably granite—marbled gray and white with flecks of black that somehow sparkled in just the right light, especially when it was slick and wet.

I'm not sure how large it was, but to me, it was huge, shaped like a ship, the stern pointing into the cold water rushing by. Flat on top—in two tiers—it also became a set of "stages" to us kids where we would act out any number of adventure stories. That rock was just as much a part of my childhood as BAND-AID–laden knees and toothless lisps.

My rock was a ship that took me far away from the harsh realities of life. It was the one place I remember that was steady. Always there. Waiting and ready to serve. Holding me no matter what was going on.

It didn't move, yet I charted my course forward on it with sails bellowed full of endless creativity and imagination powering oh-so-many childhood adventures.

Harbored in a slight bend in the creek, it was always ready to support me when I was exhausted after running from the house fueled by anger, confusion, and pain. I would seek the cool solace of its surface to hold and support me as I lay sobbing, tears cascading down my cheeks and rolling onto its surface.

As children, Maddy, Jack, and I would scurry to the ship when we didn't head to the magic bus after school. We'd gather whatever supplies we needed and follow the creek bed, gleefully navigating jutting tree roots, rocks, and the occasional woodchuck hole as skillfully as fire walkers.

The air grew thick with mosquitoes the closer we got to the creek. We didn't mind. We were on a mission. If I close my eyes right now, I can hear the annoying buzz of the bugs, the chirping of what sounded like jungle birds but were really crows, and the familiar gurgle of the creek as we passed pink and white lady's slippers standing like salacious sentries along the footpath.

Sometimes we'd be lucky enough to find a tree that had fallen at just the perfect angle to form a natural bridge to the other side of the creek. Other times, we'd craft a makeshift ferry out of a piece of metal from the junkyard, only to sink and get wet anyway.

We'd eventually get to our destination. Our rock. It had one pointy edge jutting out into the creek as if it were a ship momentarily docked and ready to launch for parts unknown.

Often we made it our pirate ship, complete with one-legged pirates expertly navigating it through rough open seas—after narrowly escaping angry island cannibals, of course—being sore losers after their dinner ran with their treasures. Or it became the soundstage for a new Tarzan and Jane flick. We'd cajole someone—most likely Jack—into climbing a not-so-safe creekside tree to grab one of the thick, coarse purple vines hanging down from its branches and beg him to jump and swing—bellowing that repetitive rhythm of the deep throaty singsong Tarzan call, "Aah-eeh-ah-eeh-aaaaaah-eeh-ah-eeh-aaaaah," echoing in the woods. The vine would often break, and the film scene would abruptly end.

The scenarios that played out on the rock got real as I got older. It was the place I'd race to when I couldn't take it anymore. I threw myself on its chilly, slick surface; my body racked with emotion as my heart burst open, raw, exposed, and wounded.

I'd race to the rock, clutching my softcover Flower Power diary. I'd arrive at my safe place feeling like I'd traveled for miles, heave my body onto the rock, open my diary, and let the words feverishly come. My emotions were liquid, flowing page after page from my favorite pen—the one with the cap jagged from teeth marks—until the tears slowed down and eventually stopped.

I wrote about what was happening to me. The pressure to keep silent. Inappropriate touches slowly stealing any traces left of childhood innocence. Then, as I was growing older, the confusion of being abandoned, not wanted. Fear that I did something wrong. Was there something wrong with me?

I wrote about Mr. P. and me. I wrote about things a typical preteen would. How unfair life was. How confusing my emotions and my life were. My hopes and dreams. Fantasies. Working through the confusion and my thoughts with words worked. It was safe. I could allow the push-pull tug of it all to sort itself out on the page.

I wrote words asking the "whys" I couldn't ask. Words exploring emotions and sensations I had difficulty describing. Words sharing secrets I couldn't dare share with anyone, especially my best friend Robin, who lived the perfect life with her perfectly loving parents in the perfect house nestled on a perfectly manicured lawn.

One thing I knew was that I couldn't tell my parents. Even as a child—and later a teen—I understood the potential ramifications of this truth. The truth was that I had to handle all my problems myself. If I ever told my parents about Mr. P, I knew my dad's anger would take over. I knew he would grab the 22 in the back-right side of his bedroom closet and end it. I knew that telling would put my life at greater risk than keeping it to myself. I imagined our future being even worse if Dad went to prison as a murderer. We'd be alone and even poorer. I understood I'd have to write it down to get it out. I could handle the truth, and my dad couldn't.

I held my secrets just like that rock held me.

After my written confession, I always felt relief. I'd roll onto my back, feeling the grounded rock supporting me. Then, with my eyes wide open, I could begin to see. There it was. The robin egg blue sky peeking out from a break in the fluffy clouds. The sweet melody the birds were singing to me, and I could breathe. I felt cleansed as the water gurgled and ran over the rocks in the creek bed until the jagged, rough surfaces were as smooth as glass.

Bright Lights Hiding Shadows

I STARE INTO THE DIRTY MIRROR THAT STRETCHES ACROSS THE ENTIRE WALL above multiple pink sinks in the girls' locker room. The aroma of sweat, Aqua Net, and Love's Baby Soft swirled around me.

Gripping the sink with my hands, I tried to steady myself. *You can do this. You've got to do this.*

I take a deep breath. I stare at my determined and nervous fourteen-year-old, tiny and pale face with almond-shaped glasses covering what future boyfriends would call the most bottomless blue eyes they'd ever seen. Mousy brown hair hung past my shoulders, the white of my scalp down my middle part, marking me as a potential Addams family member. I am wearing my favorite striped turtleneck, which I had been sure was identical to Jan's on a recent episode of *The Brady Bunch*.

My stomach somersaulted as the voice inside inquired, *Do I have to pee again? Oh, are my palms actually sweaty? Hey, do palms even sweat? Do we really have sweat glands there? Why am I doing this?*

I was about to return to the bathroom stall when Robin burst in, her long blonde hair flying, jolting me back to reality. "Laurie, you're up next. Come on!"

The spell broken, I grabbed my guitar, making sure my pick was still nestled between the thin wire strings, and walked out into the cinderblock hallway that led to the "big" gymnasium.

The Haddam Killingworth High School was still putting the finishing touches on a new auditorium, so that year, our musical concert was being held in the "big" gymnasium lined with pull-out bleachers and a brand-new digital scoreboard suspended from the ceiling.

My music teacher, Mr. Howell, looked relieved when he saw me coming. After all, he was the reason I was even doing this. Earlier that year, he gently urged me to join the special chorus. From that moment on, I lost myself in song every Wednesday after school.

Mr. Howell's hand warmly patted my back to calm me, sending mini-shock waves through me as he said something I didn't hear. I grinned and pulled away, placing my genuine Mexican macramé strap over my head so the guitar was across my chest. He nodded approvingly and gently pushed me toward a small opening in the makeshift curtain the janitorial crew had set up so we'd have a backdrop to our "stage."

I walked on autopilot for what felt like a mile toward the single tall wooden stool set up just where it had been when we rehearsed the day before. But this time, in front of that stool were rows and rows of metal chairs with people in them. Hundreds of people watched me walk toward the stool across the gleaming wooden gym floors.

Gulp. My heart beat so loudly that I thought the mic would pick it up. I was sure everyone could feel it, too. Awkwardly, I climbed up on top of that stool, struggling a bit with my big guitar. I positioned my Fender guitar pick and looked into the audience filled with expectant faces—grandparents, moms, dads, and classmates.

I saw my family sitting just off to my right. Just as I had expected, Mom was sitting next to Cindy, Ryan, Maddy, and then Jack, who I could see was squirming a bit to see over the person sitting in front of him. Then I saw Dad in one of his worn blue work shirts, and my heart opened a bit. He usually wasn't into this type of thing, but there he was, sitting uncomfortably in the straight metal chair.

I took a breath, bent my head to the guitar, and then it happened.

I don't know how or why, but it does.

I am no longer the junkyard girl. The one that wears clothes her mom makes. The girl from *that* side of town. The girl with secrets.

I am The Performer. Someone glossy. Special. And I sing, strum, and belt out, "Jeremiah was a bullfrog. . . ." Some might say I belted out those words as if my life depended on it. They would be so very right.

And then everyone was clapping. People were smiling and leaping up and cheering. Dad standing taller than I'd ever seen him. Mom was beside him, her face beaming. Even Maddy was smiling and clapping wildly. All that noise and applause was for me.

They liked it. They liked me. I was okay.

Later that week, Mom was having coffee with her best friend Nancy at our kitchen table, and I overheard Nancy say, "Glory, when she stepped up on the big stool with that huge guitar that looked bigger than her, I wasn't sure what to expect. But when she opened her mouth to sing, I couldn't believe the sound that came out of little Laurie. Who would have known? It was quite a surprise."

Mom smiled and sipped her coffee, hands holding the mug for warmth. She wasn't surprised. She knew what I had in me.

Performing—music and theater—became a big part of my survival. It was how I felt safe enough to meet life head-on.

Years later, as a lowly freshman at Marist College, The Performer got the role of Puck in *A Midsummer Night's Dream*.

Clever, conniving Puck pranced or lurked on stage in almost every scene, delivering lines of medieval poetry. Puck was a changeling, becoming whatever he or she needed to be.

I was born for that part.

To survive as a misfit—much like Puck—I ducked and dodged truths behind a façade, showing people only what I wanted them to see. Striving with every creative word and action to gain approval—to be okay. Even I believed the stories I wove. I became a shiny version of myself, the junkyard girl banished from view for not being enough.

Despite the shame I carried, the performer craved the spotlight. I needed it, not to feel special but to feel normal. The brighter the light shining on me—the easier it was to pretend and push the shadows deeper inside.

It wasn't until later in life I realized I had to find a way to bring those shadows back up and into the light. I learned how to meet those shadows and invite them out onto the stage of my life with me.

The Open Road Ahead

WHILE MANY OF MY FELLOW 1979 GRADUATES OF HADDAM KILLINGWORTH HIGH School were already sitting in the passenger seats of service vans beginning trade apprenticeships, practicing cut and curl styles atop Styrofoam mannequins or laying underneath hoisted cars while learning the difference between an alternator, starter, and timing belt, I was packing my suitcase.

To this day, an empty suitcase fills me. It's full of what is to come—travel, movement, and exploration of an unknown. That hot summer day in August, my battered suitcase was an open invitation to discover who I really was.

Carefully considering what to bring, I had no idea how much I desperately needed to leave behind.

Earlier that year, I had ripped open the large envelope containing the acceptance letter from Marist College. Thanks to a scholarship, I had been invited to join the class of 1983.

Mom and I had spent months purchasing essentials from the list Marist College provided. As I carefully packed my brand-new toiletries, arranged neatly in a practical plastic shower caddy, and folded some of my new clothes—still sporting tags that proved they weren't secondhand or homemade, I began to set aside other dorm necessities in my "to take" box. These included the geometric patterned sheets and coordinated red and beige reversible, machine-washable comforter we had ordered from the JCPenney catalog, my coveted stereo, my LP collection, and a stack of treasured, well-read books.

With freshman orientation a week away, I counted the days and hours.

Knowing my days at home were limited, I scanned my messy bedroom, seeking items to pack. Hope rose as my mind wandered. A vision of ME supplanted one of the happy-go-lucky college co-eds I had dreamingly studied on the glossy cover of the Marist College Class of 1983 welcome brochure. I had spent so much time scanning its pages for hints of what to expect that they were creased and starting to fall apart from the seam.

I had some college campus experience, visiting my high school boyfriend at UCONN, yet my first actual step on the Marist campus—my college campus—would come the following week.

Marist, located in the Mid-Hudson Valley of New York, was about a two-and-a-half-hour car ride from my house. I'd never been to New York, and although the photos depicted older buildings dotted among sprawling green spaces overlooking the Hudson River, I imagined my new city life. I was going to live in New York!

Holding my HK yearbook, I paused to figure out where to stuff it. I smiled, anticipating the lifelong friends I would make in college. But my imagination didn't stop there as I began to see my future—invited to fabulous weddings, baby showers, and all that would come from my about-to-unfold adult life.

Lost in an inner montage of "this is your future college life, Laurie," I saw a happier, more well-adjusted version of myself quickly having meaningful and intellectually stimulating conversations with classmates as we casually strolled across the campus green, textbooks in hand. I could hear the clever banter, surrounded by my circle of friends, as we toasted to our future in the Marist Ratskeller pub or danced the night away, carefree at a frat party off-campus. Things would be so different. Finally, I'd have a chance to be normal. No one would know me as the junkyard girl.

I looked down and noticed my HK yearbook—filled with memories and heartfelt quotes from my closest friends. I didn't skip a beat as I tossed it on the floor to be left with many of those friends.

Something inside me loosened. A minuscule crack appeared, allowing a sliver of light to escape. This small fissure would eventually join others that had appeared in similar moments in my past. Such as, when lost in the music, I would sing and strum my guitar without a care about who was listening. Or that euphoric feeling I felt the first time my hands wound around the steering wheel, speeding all by myself down the highway toward the beach, windows open, car speakers blaring. I was bursting with happiness and joy by singing at the top of my lungs to a mixed tape I had recorded of Casey Kasem's American Top 40 countdown radio show. Staring straight ahead at the open road ahead, I was going somewhere.

Oxygen

I DON'T REMEMBER EXACTLY WHEN WE KNEW SHE WAS SICK. LOOKING BACK, I realize there were signs. She always had that raspy voice as if she were gasping for air between words. I don't recall when I noticed how hard it was for her to catch her breath. Or that she was repeating herself. Or forgetfulness. It was a slow progression, losing her bit by bit as her brain was deprived of the oxygen it needed to function properly.

I can't imagine what that must feel like. *Was Mom aware that something was wrong? How could she not? Or was she hiding the truth because she knew something was terribly wrong and couldn't face it?* It was just one more hurdle put in front of her—of our family. One more thing she had to fight against.

Our short phone conversations from the pay phone in my dorm hall were nothing unusual. Mom's scratchy voice peppered predictable questions punctuated with a few occasional coughing spells—nothing unusual. "Laurie, how are you doing in school? You need anything? How's the food?" Occasionally, she'd fill me in on what Jack and Maddy were up to. But the calls were usually quick; they were long distance, after all.

Coughing was like white noise in our house. There was always a chorus of coughing coming from behind my parent's closed bedroom door or accompanying that first cup of coffee and, yes, first cigarette of the morning. I never really noticed it. Until I had reason to.

I was away at college, rightly self-absorbed in creating my new life. Slowly, I noticed Mom wasn't on top of things like she used to be. All of us found ourselves repeating stuff we'd already told her. She seemed at a loss for words—something my mom never was!

Usually, she took care of paying all the bills (or at least holding them off for payment for as long as necessary). She managed household budgets, prioritizing what we needed within what we had. Our health insurance bill was always one of the bills she found a way to pay—knowing that at any moment, something could happen to Dad in the yard, and he could need some medical care or one of us kids might need to go to the doctor. I don't remember Mom ever going to the doctor—but that was about to change.

It was a time of change—with me going to college—and Dad selling the junkyard so he and Mom could move into a smaller *new* house about a thousand yards up from the junkyard on the top of Watson Hill.

Did Dad somehow know that Mom would need a smaller single-story home? Did he have a premonition?

Mom was so excited to get the new house. It was a beauty, too—a prefab modular home that came to us directly from the factory on two large tractor-trailers. It was to be put together like a snap-on toy. Polaroid shots depicted the front and back of the house split down the middle, resting on blocks before they lowered it onto the cinderblock foundation that had been dug and prepared for its arrival. It was like peering into a life-sized version of my best friend Robin's dollhouse her dad had made her—except honestly, her dollhouse had more rooms and was better furnished.

As Dad was in the process of selling the junkyard, Mom was to organize cleaning out the house and moving what we wanted to keep. I had come home for the weekend to help sort through things. Maddy and I carefully went through our room, deciding what to bring. I boxed up my treasured collection of Nancy Drew mysteries; I had the complete set. I piled them into a box as I dreamed of the daughter I would have one day to gift them to and recalled all the outings with Grandma Martinez, where she bought each book for me.

Maddy and I argued a bit over which Barbies were whose. Eventually, we settled up. I packed up the cardboard box Malibu beach house, Ginger, a few crazy-haired Barbies scantily clad, and oodles of home-made miniature outfits Mom had made. I remember gingerly packing those outfits—miniature dresses with tiny zippers and matching dress coats and miniskirts in wild patterns made from remnants of Mom's many sewing projects. Feeling nostalgic and grown up, I labeled each box KEEP—LAURIE'S STUFF and set it aside. We also boxed books, toys, and other items we no longer wanted and labeled those DONATE.

Months later, I realized Mom had mixed up those boxes and kept the wrong ones. Hopefully, someone else somewhere was enjoying my complete set of Nancy Drew and the beautifully crafted Barbie clothes my mom painstakingly made. Downstairs, nestled in our new basement, lay boxes of junk we didn't want. Arghhhhhhh. We had brought the junkyard with us.

Was it a sign of the mess that was to come?

Mom certainly didn't mean to do it. That mix-up was the least of our family's worries. Mom had also thought she had paid bills when she hadn't. Unfortunately, after she had been diagnosed with emphysema, we discovered that she had also let our health insurance lapse. Her illness had been causing symptoms she never mentioned, including chest pain, shortness of breath, foggy brain, and memory loss due to lack of oxygen.

The severity of the diagnosis didn't really hit me because, in the beginning, she didn't seem sick. She was Mom. The same strong person, puffing on cigarettes, sipping coffee, freshly painted red fingernails surrounding her cup. Yet, as time went by, I increased the frequency of my visits home. With each visit, she moved more slowly. Her skin became ashen, her breathing more labored. And eventually, I came home to find an oxygen machine in the hallway, allowing her to go around the house only as far as the thin plastic air tube could reach.

I couldn't have kept going if that had been me. After all she had been through with Dad, all the money struggles, the heartache, the pushing at life to make it—wouldn't it be easier just to give up?

The only thing more challenging than her struggle to live was her nicotine addiction. I remember the only time she'd take the oxygen mask off her face was to walk far enough from the combustible machine to light up another cigarette. She saw me watching her and said with defeat, "I know, Laurie. But this relaxes me, and I need it."

Sometimes, the things we need kill us.

I think I had known that those cigarettes would be the end of her. I was in fourth or fifth grade when I started my anti-smoking campaign at home after seeing the "Nicotine—The Silent Killer" film in health class. I couldn't understand why Mom and Dad continued to smoke when they knew it would kill them. I would fill ashtrays with water so cigarettes left resting there would get wet and go out—soaked and unable to be relit. I'd empty complete packs of ciga-rettes, leaving notes inside saying, "Please don't smoke" or "Just quit." I had no idea about addiction and how powerful it was.

Eventually, I knew I wouldn't win and let my parents be.

Why is it that when we know we are losing someone, we allow ourselves to notice their importance, the role they steadily played behind the scenes, and to see the hole that will be there without them?

Mom was always there—always in our corner—my corner. She was stronger than she appeared. Yet, her body wasn't strong enough to keep going without oxygen.

Growing up, Mom was my oxygen, but I didn't know that back then. Seeing and experiencing her strength—her continued fight to make life "normal" for us, fueled the part of me that knew I'd make it.

I did make it, and I wish she were here so I could thank her for all she did for us. Show my gratitude by buying her a beautiful home and making her life easier and much more comfortable so she could let down her guard and give up some of the fight. Rest and breathe easier.

In reality, Mom never gave up the fight. She fought for each breath as she battled emphysema. She died at age fifty-seven, shortly after I married.

Oh, Chica!

I AWOKE TO THE PUTRID SMELL AND SWEET/SOUR TASTE OF VOMIT IN MY DRY mouth. Gross, I thought as I tried to lift my head, which felt like a 20-ton boulder. I gave up without really lifting anything at all.

I wasn't going anywhere, yet my mind was racing.

Lying there for I don't know how long, I slowly opened my eyes and could see that I was indeed—thankfully—fully dressed, covers twisted around my legs and torso, and in my own dorm room staring at my digital clock, which I think read 11:45? a.m.? p.m.? While my body still felt like it was last night, my mind slowly wrapped around the fact that it was approaching noon as I realized the sun was shining through the window above my desk.

I closed my eyes at the unwanted brightness; my mind was fuzzy, yet my body determined to get up. I started to move my head and quickly and gently set it back down. *Whoa. Easy, Nelly,* I thought as the room spun uncontrollably. *Oh, no. . . . What did you do, Laurie? What did you do?*

Vague snippets of the night before began to come to me as I lay there motionless.

I remember getting ready to go out in anticipation of the night ahead. The Go-Go's—"We Got the Beat"—blaring from the LP spinning on my stereo, body bopping as I did my best to finish my makeup: blood-red lips and heavy black eyeliner. Spiking my short hair on top of my head just like Annie Lennox from the Eurythmics, I was gearing up for a fun night with "my guys" at the Ratskeller, our on-campus pub.

Yes, I had a "date" with eight guys. Yup, eight guys from the boat I was coxswain for. We had all been training hard for the upcoming regatta, and I had promised to meet them all to celebrate. After running, weight lifting, and so many practice rounds in the "tanks," they all had "made weight" for our boat class.

My eyes closed, and I may have rested a bit more when a memory woke me.

I was downing a beer and slamming the glass on the table—foam spilling as I grabbed another full glass next to it. Chants of "chug, chug. . ." surrounded me as I downed the second glass. What? Me? Accepting a drinking challenge from, wait—was that really Josh from the football team? Cheers, drinks, and more cheers. *Oh my, what HAD I done?* No wonder my head hurt.

I don't know what happened. I rarely allowed myself to get like this. I was usually the responsible one. Despite the fact we were all legal drinking age back then, I rarely drank—and definitely never too much. This simply wasn't me. I would slowly sip my beer—or my new favorite, a fuzzy navel—sip by sip, while observing everyone else getting hammered and doing things they would regret the following morning. I was one of the few who remembered what they did. I'd always watch for my girlfriends and ensure they didn't get in dangerous situations. I was the one always on alert—at the ready—to orchestrate getting someone safely home and tucked in bed, wastebasket at the ready.

I finally made it in and out of the shower, stopping every minute to hang onto the shower stall wall to steady myself. Thankfully, I was no longer sick, but the stink on the heap of clothes piled on the floor, and the awful taste in my mouth told me I had been at some point last night (or was it this morning?).

Slinking down the stairs, I had a new mission to reach the cafeteria across campus to snag something to eat before lunch service was over.

I knew all the lunch ladies (and a few gents that worked there, too) because I delivered their mail during my day job in the campus post office. They often let me grab a cookie just out of the massive shiny commercial ovens—offering the rare treat of eating one of their mass-manufactured desserts freshly baked on a hot tray. I quickly learned that was the only way to eat them, as they would be rock hard by dinner.

While I wasn't sure what to eat, I knew I had to eat something. With each step down the stairs—my stomach swirled. *Must. Get. Food.* This was my mantra with every step. I had to get something in my stomach that could both appease the upset and absorb whatever alcohol still remained in my system that must be the cause of an unfamiliar woozy feeling overcoming me in waves.

As I reached the bottom of the stairs, a sharp pain accompanied hoots and hollers from the three friends sitting in their PJs and slippers in the common area.

The three amigos were my housemates and besties. They were often the source of earthly and unfamiliar aromas from the common kitchen area, accompanied by fast-paced Spanish conversation and lots and lots of laughter. I could smell the results of their kitchen conclave, including sticky rice served with vegetables dripping with tangy golden sauces smelling spicy from curry and an unsuspected sweetness of coconut milk, pineapples, mangoes, or papaya.

Although I didn't recognize them as kitchen goddesses until later in life when I started to experiment in the kitchen myself, I fondly recall these three lovely ladies had introduced me to plantains, funny-looking banana-shaped fruits that were often cut up into chunky bite-sized pieces and fried in coconut oil. Unlike their sweet Americanized yellow cousins, plantains were meatier. They weren't mushy when made into thin chips but were subtly sweet and delicious—especially caramelized and glistening with hot oil.

"Where are you off to, sweetie?" Gina questioned, looking fresh and fine, though I knew she hadn't showered yet.

"Boy, you were quite the *chica* last night," piped in Claudine. "I didn't know you spoke Spanish."

"I what?" I retorted. "I spoke Spanish? Really? I took French in high school, not Spanish, and I barely remember that. My grandma spoke Spanish to me as a kid, though. Maybe I somehow remembered it? Weird."

Pausing to lean on the arm of the couch, I held my hand across my stomach to rest.

"Yes, we were in the kitchen last night when we heard you moaning. We helped you honor the porcelain god, ensuring you didn't miss the bowl. You almost threw up in the hallway, where we found you muttering Spanish," said Gina. "It would have been funny except we'd never seen you come home like that, and you were so sick. Sweetie, you feelin' okay?"

"Must have been quite a night, Laurie," added Claudine, making that tsk-tsk sound but smiling at me, seeking more details.

"I have a feeling I don't even know half of it," I said as I continued toward the door. "Thanks for helping me last night. Sorry, I don't remember."

"Hey, we were happy to help. Hope you get to the café before lunch ends."

I stumbled out the door, blinded by the light and the realization that I had no idea what happened last night. This was my worst nightmare.

I had promised myself I would never let my guard down and get so drunk I wasn't in control. I had to be in the driver's seat, knowing what was going on, what was about to happen, and who I was with—really knowing who they were.

I rarely let myself be so free to trust another person with my whole self. I was afraid of what I would do or say, or who I would be. I could not let that happen.

The realization I had no idea what I had done made me feel immediately sick—but not from the overabundance of alcohol I had obviously consumed. I was feverish as a twisted, dark gnawing grew deep inside me. I felt sick to the core—not knowing with certainty all the details of what had happened last night.

I was off my game. I couldn't lose control. Yet, I had.

Why was it that there wasn't ever anyone watching over me?

Shaken Not Stirred

DESPITE MR. P AND EVERYTHING HE TOOK FROM ME, I DON'T WISH I'D HAD A different childhood.

There are so many happy—even magical—memories that make up for the ones that aren't. That makes me who I am today.

Our first-ever family vacation is a good example.

I was eight or nine and thrilled to be going to the Catskill Game Farm. I remember hoping the farm would sell postcards so I could send one to my best friend as positive proof we were a normal family going on holiday.

Mom had loaded us three younger kids in the back of the sky-blue Buick. My older siblings Cindy and Ryan weren't there—perhaps they had summer jobs. Dad, hair slicked back with a fresh application of Brylcreem, got behind the wheel. "Did you grab the cash?" he asked Mom, cigarette butt bobbing from his lower lip as he spoke.

"Well, no, I didn't, Bob," she said, slightly slumping in the front seat. "I wasn't sure where to look. And besides, I couldn't find the shovel."

Dad didn't miss a beat. He exited the car, walked to the garage, and emerged with a small rusted-out shovel a minute later. We kids peeked out the back window, jostling each other as we pushed aside our "suit-cases"—paper grocery bags overflowing with clothes, shoes, and other trip necessities—so we could see.

Our eyes followed Dad as he approached the small pine tree near the house. He turned his back to us and started purposefully walking, counting out a certain number of paces from the base of the tree. Suddenly, he stopped, took a drag from his cig, glanced around, and started to dig.

I wasn't sure if Mom was annoyed or bored, but she lit another cigarette as she tilted the rearview mirror to watch Dad without turning around.

In what seemed like no time, Dad returned to the car holding a blue Maxwell House coffee can covered with dark and damp clay soil. He handed the can to Mom and turned back to us kids. His fake teeth gleaming, he said, "Okey dokey. You guys ready to feed some deer right out of the palm of your hand?"

Dad never trusted putting our money in the bank and didn't like paying taxes. Thanks to the junkyard being a cash business, our bank was an old buried coffee can. With the tires spinning gravel, off we went on our first-ever vacation bankrolled by the wad of cash he had literally unearthed.

That was the trip of a lifetime for us. We ate at Howard Johnson's, stayed at a real motel, and, as Dad predicted, we did feed wild forest animals, including several soft speckled baby deer weird-smelling pellet food Mom bought at a hut with a grass roof. We aimlessly walked with the other families in a large, penned area where the animals roamed around looking for handouts from us—the paying guests.

We got up close and personal with fat black, brown, and pinkish hogs, baby fawns—and I guess mama and daddy deer. My little brother Jack kept calling the ones with antlers Reindeer, and no one corrected him.

We also saw a dancing bear with a baby black bear and some pretty old donkeys that looked super sad. If you paid extra (we didn't), you could hold and feed a baby lamb with a bottle.

Maddy, Mom, and I put our faces through funny wooden cutouts of a farmer, his wife, and a cow, and Jack got scared when one of the reindeer almost mistook his tiny fingers for some food.

Overall, I have warm memories of us being an almost typical family—laughing, bickering in the car with Jack and Maddy over stupid stuff like who had to sit in the middle, seeing my parents together like a couple, and being another family on vacation.

It's memories like this that cancel out the bad ones. All my memories—from suppressed to fuzzy to crystal clear—collectively created my custom recipe for who I am. Well, maybe it wasn't a recipe that would require particular ingredients—more like a collection of events that somehow gave me the resilience and skills to survive and eventually thrive. Kinda like someone else. . . .

The first time I saw 007 was on the big screen at the drive-in. I think it was *Diamonds Are Forever*. I have many memories of going to the drive-in. They offered one price for a packed car, and we could easily bring our own snacks. I often brought my shiny pleather wallet and used some of my precious babysitting money to spring for one of those big popcorn buckets with the delicious liquid "butter" they squirted from a canister on the counter.

I was watching from the backseat. Due to the poor quality of the crackling audio from the rusted-out speaker box precariously hanging from our car window and the fact that I frequently had to defend my precious popcorn from Maddy and Jack grabbing handfuls at a time, I missed bits of the plot. So when James Bond asked for his martini to be prepared that particular Bond way, I took its meaning differently.

My brain was working in overdrive as I saw him smile at the camera, all smug and debonair as if proclaiming he—not just his martini—was "shaken not stirred" by his adventures. How could he do that after all the chaos that had just happened to and around him?

I watched in awe as he scaled the walls of the secret lab, maneuvered his fast car around Las Vegas, avoiding the police and the bad guys, and used a top-secret electronic gadget to pretend to be someone else. How deftly he managed anything that came his way. He was calm, cool, and collected as he sipped his drink in the oh-so-fancy glass and settled in to make the moves on his lady at the end of the film.

I admired his ability to navigate disaster and any challenge that came his way. I remember thinking, *That's me. I'm shaken not stirred. Ready to take on whatever comes next.*

PART FOUR

Diamonds in the Dirt

Cracks That Let the Light In

"THERE IS A CRACK. . .THAT'S HOW THE LIGHT GETS IN."—LEONARD COHEN

The drive to campus to start my freshman year at Marist was filled with anxiety and exhilaration. It was just me, Dad, and Mom. Cindy and Ryan had said their goodbyes earlier that week. Maddy and Jack stayed behind after an awkward hug in our dirt driveway. I felt pensive as I waved out the window, leaving them behind, but that feeling evaporated along with the dust cloud that slowly settled after Dad peeled our overpacked Impala out of the driveway.

This was momentous: I don't think I'd ever gone anywhere with just Mom and Dad, and they would return home without me.

I could tell Dad was nervous.

The car carrying Mom, Dad, and me hurling toward Marist began to make an odd noise that seemed to get louder and louder as we continued west beyond Hartford. Dad said he'd have to check the car muffler when we arrived. I dizzily watched homes, farms, factories, and cities spin by, listening to the noisy soundtrack of the muffler, my face blasted by warm air from the open window. Hurling toward my destiny in Poughkeepsie, New York, another crack opens.

Dad would fill some of the silences with odd and not-so-funny comments, such as saying the drive was taking so long he and Mom wouldn't have time to do more than kick me out at the curb. He was muttering about how they couldn't be "late" for an "important appointment" back home—meeting friends to celebrate getting rid of me at The Tavern, the local hole-in-the-wall bar downtown.

He told me in detail how he had a plan for an expedient and efficient drop-off. Dad was an inventor and often devised plans for all sorts of things. This time, he said this would be a "drop me off" as he'd pull up the old Impala to the front gates at Marist and slow down just a wee bit enough to let me open the door and jump out curbside. His voice rose to a crescendo as he declared it. Yet, he must have thought things over a bit more because he quibbled a few minutes later, "Well, I guess we will have to stop. Otherwise, we won't be able to toss out all your 'loot' on the sidewalk with you."

The thing with Dad was that you never knew if he was joking or not. He'd followed through on some crazy plans in the past, like the time he said Mom deserved some flowers, and the following day some hastily uprooted flowering bushes were lying on their side—with Connecticut clay still clinging to their exposed underbellies—an exact match to the muddy dirt sticking to the tire treads in his car and the holes in our neighbor's front lawn.

So let's just say I spent more than a few minutes in the back seat sweating it out that he was actually serious.

Thankfully, he wasn't. Yet that didn't save the drop-off from being bizarre.

None of us in the car had ever done anything like this. For all I knew, Dad had never stepped foot on a college campus, let alone deposited a daughter there. All of us were trying our best not to appear out of our element—yet clearly, we were.

Dad was sporting his best navy work pants. And by work pants, I mean the kind you see service men wearing—not pants you'd wear with a suit and tie. I was thankful he wasn't wearing the usual matching work shirt with "Bob" engraved in gold script over the pocket. Giving him the once over, he did look good. He was handsome, with his thin, angular face accentuated by his bright blue eyes twinkling with either nervousness or excitement—maybe a little of both. His pants were actually clean, and he wore a regular button-up shirt. (Thanks, Mom!) His tall, slender silhouette was spoiled just a bit by a protruding mini pot belly—in its infant stage—hanging just over his belt.

Noticing his gleaming smile and slicked-back hair as he exited the car to stretch dramatically, I realized he was making an effort just for me. He had obviously put in his teeth, generally reserved for weddings and funerals. (Dad used to joke that we didn't have to put them in for his funeral—and I don't think we did.)

Mom patted her hair down and put on some lipstick. Stepping out of the car to stand beside our beater of a car, she glanced around at the crowded parking lot, looking nervous but poised and collected—maybe even proud.

We all watched as we took in the scene before us. Families busily unload cars and carry boxes, suitcases, stereo equipment, rugs, and standing lights up a long flight of steps toward the dorms towering above. Watching Mom and those around us, I sensed she shared my excitement to be a part of all this. Of course, she did. Mom was there the afternoon I opened the envelope that had come for me back in May. She hugged me and watched me dance around the kitchen when I read the acceptance letter informing me of the scholarship that made today possible.

Catching me looking at her, she smiled and said, "Okay, Laurie. Let's go on up and see what we need to do. Come on, Bob."

After finding the Red Fox Class of '83 check-in table, with the help of a few friendly campus guides, we eventually found my dorm room. Leo Floor 4. Room 407. Wow. I was here. I opened the door, hoping to find my roommate Sylvia from New York City. She wasn't there but had already moved in, as one side of the room sported a lovely flowered comforter, a few potted plants, some family photos in picture frames, and a fabulous shaggy rug.

Hours later, after bringing up my things from the car and taking a campus tour, complete with eating ice cream sundaes in the Student Union, I could tell Dad was getting itchy to return home. The walk back to the car felt sooooo long and awkward. I wanted to admit I'd miss them, but I was oh-so-ready to be free.

When I finally said goodbye, Mom gave me some last-minute advice—something about calling collect if I needed to—and told me to write. Then she turned around and nervously popped into the passenger side seat, leaving Dad standing there with me. Combing his fingers through his hair, he bent down, hugged me tightly, and whispered, "Well, be good, kiddo. You know I love ya."

With that, I watched them back out of the parking space and drive away, listening to the sound of the loud muffler get fainter and fainter the farther away it went. With tears and determination, I steadily walked up the steep stairs—ones I would climb so many times throughout my four years at Marist—climbing up toward the sun's light, peeking through a crack in the clouds.

Finding My Swing

I WAKE UP TO THE SOUND OF THE ALARM BUZZING AND SHUT IT OFF QUICKLY SO AS not to wake Sylvia, sleeping just a few feet from me in our dorm room. I would often wake up just before the alarm went off. I'd lay there nestled in my cocoon of a bed in a familiar half-waking, half-sleeping haze, unsure of where I was. Sometimes, I'd get confused, and a bolt of fear would grab hold of me, but that was happening less and less.

This morning, I slowly opened my eyes—blurry vision adjusting to note the time on the large illuminated numbers on the digital alarm clock. I hit the off button and reached for my glasses; the room suddenly became focused as I put them on. Registering where I was, the thought came to me in an energetic flash of clarity. I had to get up. I couldn't be late. They depended on me.

I literally jumped out of bed. Jumping out is the only way I could get my 97-pound, 4-foot-11-and-1/4-inch body out of that too-tall bed. You should have seen how I had to get in. I looked like a pole vaulter making a running start to get high enough to get up in it. I knew I needed a small step stool, but my pride prevented me from buying one.

Shuffling to the bathroom down the hall with my plastic tote, I knew I was again the only one up. I flicked on the overhead lights that made anyone looking in the bathroom mirrors appear as pale as a vampire. The lights buzzed loudly as we both got ready to face the day.

Before I knew it, I was running toward the river, my feet finding the well-worn path down the hill in the dark. I arrived to find my guys mumbling a faint hello, moving slowly as they gathered the oars and prepared to get the shell in the water by the dock.

Coach, clipboard and coffee in hand, was getting the motor boat ready at the launch and making room for a few of the guys not starting out in the eight-man boat. They filed in like ducks in a row to sit with Coach, hoping to get a turn in a seat.

I herded the guys toward the hanger, grabbed the megaphone head-gear off the peg by its worn leather strap, and gave the commands to lift the boat and launch. Minutes later, I was settled deep down in my seat in the stern, facing eyeball to eyeball with number 8, my stroke man. He was barely awake but still managed a sheepish grin. I wondered what he had been up to last night.

After adjustments were made, we fell into that familiar rhythm, glid-ing and slicing through the cool mist rising from the water and the sun. The sky brightened slowly with each stroke as if set on a dimmer switch.

Coach barked a few drill orders from his mechanical bullhorn while his echo reminded us what to do. Eventually, we hit our stride midway through the Power 10 I've called. This is the command coxswains use to count down ten very powerful strokes.

It was then I felt it. We all did. The "swing." I'd hear from experi-enced rowers that this is the poetry of rowing. The moment when the boat feels like it is moving on its own, flying above the water. We are fluid, gracefully moving between the pulls of the oars. The boat is part of us, and we are part of it, moving in unison.

I was awake. Alive. I was the coxswain. I was the one in control. I was at peace.

This is the moment I have trouble articulating whenever anyone asks me why I joined the crew team. This is one of the reasons why I get up before sunrise five or six days a week to steer a narrow boat in fog, rain, sleet, or even sometimes, in the early spring, snow.

Another is that, well, I was asked. I was sought out.

I didn't know what crew was when I noticed that tall, muscular, blonde upperclassman standing with a few other god-like creatures across the gym early in my freshman year. Was he real? He looked too perfect to be.

I had no idea what I would be in for when I saw him walk toward me. As soon as he started walking toward me and I realized he was walking toward me, I knew I wouldn't say no to whatever he asked.

He didn't ask my name. He smiled, exposing his perfect, orthodontically corrected white teeth, looked down directly into my eyes, and asked, "How much do you weigh?"

I would have thought it was a weird question if I hadn't been stunned by his beauty. I think I managed to stammer back an answer, "Um, about ninety-seven pounds." He laughed, said that would do, and probably said something witty, to which I have no idea what I said back. He then asked if I'd consider joining the crew team. "You'd be a perfect coxswain and get to travel to regattas and party with us," he said, eyes twinkling almost as much as his smile.

Despite not knowing what the hell crew was, I was in the tanks the following week. It was where the guys could practice and perfect their rowing skills when being on the water was impossible. The tanks became my new library. It was where I got to know the different strokes and race strategies and understand the vital role of the coxswain. It was where I took on a new persona. The one who directs and becomes the boat's eyes, ears, and mouth. The person the coach relies on to implement the race plan and adjust it on the fly if necessary.

I learned that while the rowers are the power behind the boat, the coxswain is in control once a race begins. I am the only one who can talk to the rowers (via the megaphone strapped to my face) and let them know where we are in relation to the other boats, how much farther we have until the finish, and fire them up to give it their all, especially when they have nothing left. I steered the rudder and kept us in our lane to avoid race penalties. I was in charge.

I remember my first few times out on the water. Coach had me try a four-man, and eventually, I led an eight-man. They were mine. I was theirs. It was like having eight big brothers instantly. I would also learn that as the season wore on, I was responsible for supporting and encouraging my guys to do whatever it took to "make weight" and essentially keep emotions in check before and during a race. I was the den mother to eight guys. I loved it.

That first season, we had spring training in Virginia, and when we left, I had no idea that in just a few weeks, I would find myself at the center of a major campus story. It would even be covered in *The Circle*, our student newspaper—the newspaper I was hoping to write for eventually. This was not how I had planned to get the editor's attention!

Coach had given me a brand new eight-man boat that morning for practice. I am not sure what he was thinking giving me that new boat. He later regretted it.

The boat had never been in the water. It was a brand-spankin' new Kaschper fiberglass shell some prestigious alum had purchased for Marist. It was to be christened by the donors on the Marist College Homecoming Weekend, but Coach wanted us to launch it and get used to it. She was a beauty—long and sleek. The guys were excited to try it out. I was nervous.

We were out on the water first thing that morning, as usual. It was one of my first encounters crewing an eight-man on the water. The fog was heavy, but Coach told me to lead them in a power exercise. I saw what appeared to be a branch sticking out of the water to our port side, so I steered away from it. As we were gaining momentum and gliding parallel to it, we jerked to a sudden stop. Oars popped up in the air after being abruptly stopped. I don't remember if any of the guys caught a crab and flew out of the boat. We heard a big loud crack. Shit. We had hit something big and solid.

With Coach yelling through the bullhorn, panic ensued in the boat. We were taking on water fast. We were sinking.

I don't remember what happened next. It's a convenient blur. I remember calling my mom from a payphone that night and telling her I had broken a brand-new boat. "Mom, I've got to quit. I can't do this. I don't belong here." I asked her to send me money to take a bus home. Mom basically held her ground and told me no. "Laurie, it was a mistake. You need to stick this out. Own your mistake and make it right." I don't think she realized what an expensive mistake it was.

This mistake would be shared once we got back to campus and take on a mythic-like quality. The new boat, the Kaschper shell, became known as the GASHper—thanks to me. At the Marist College Homecoming Alumni Weekend, they christened the boat with a decorative drape conveniently covering the damage. I was mortified. Later that season, the boat was repaired and forever bore a professionally made patch where the gash had been in the bow. From that moment on, that boat was lovingly referred to by the crew team as the GASHper.

I faced my mistake and never underestimated anything floating in the water again. In the spring, when the ice that formed along the banks of the Hudson River would slowly melt, we'd row by large icebergs formed around the most bizarre items. I learned to steer clear of these mini-icebergs, including one that enclosed a semi-thawed but preserved frozen cow, discarded kitchen appliances, tires, and even a colorful plastic kid's playhouse bobbing in the icy water.

Despite this dramatic start to my coxswain career at Marist, I was crazy about the sport and couldn't wait to be on the water. I felt in control and free at the same time. I barked orders, and as if by magic, they obeyed! As soon as we hit the water and I felt the wind in my face, it brought back being in the back of Mr. P's truck—letting it all go along with the wind. Strangely, it felt good.

At Marist, I began to find my swing on the water and in life.

Truth

AS A CHILD, I MADE UP A LOT OF STUFF. I HAD TO. I REMEMBER GETTING INTO TROU-
ble in kindergarten for telling classmates that my dad owned a chocolate
factory, and I could have all the chocolate bars I wanted—even for breakfast! (To be honest, eating chocolate for breakfast wasn't that far from the
truth. I'd often scarf down a Hostess HoHo running up the hill to catch
the school bus.)

I just wanted to be liked. Accepted. To make friends. To have the
opportunity to be a friend. But what could I really offer anyone? To play
in the dirt pile with me? Play among the cars, trucks, and derelicts that
hung around the yard?

When I lied about what my dad did that day in kindergarten, the
school called Mom. I imagine Mom just laughing it off with Dad as they
shared a cup of coffee at the kitchen table. However, as punishment, my
teacher Mrs. Dickens made me get up in front of the entire class and tell
the truth the next day. I remember it was the morning we had reviewed
Mrs. D's Ten Commandments of Being a Good Classmate. (Hint: Lying
was not one of them.)

My head, along with my long, straggly brown hair, hung over my
small body as I stood there staring at my feet. I noticed, perhaps for the
first time, the scuffed toes of my shoes compared to my classmates' new
school shoes, my voice shaking in rhythm with my body. Slowly, a weak
voice came from inside me for all to hear that my dad didn't own a chocolate factory. That I lied. The truth was that my dad owned a junkyard
that I lived right in the middle of. That I was sorry.

Kids laughed and pointed at me. It wasn't approval or friendship that I saw in their eyes. My head lowered as my brain and body registered this feeling that I would later recognize so many times in my life. I wasn't good enough.

The lack of compassion from that teacher still astounds me today. I can still feel the sting and pain of her righteous shaming of me in front of the class. I felt small and insignificant, and I was branded a liar.

Years later, the stigma of where I lived continued to influence my reputation as I would later be called "Junkyard Girl" or worse, "Junkyard Dog" if classmates wanted to be especially cruel.

You'd think the shame I experienced that day in kindergarten would have stopped me from telling more lies or stretching the truth. But it didn't. I learned that telling the truth is painful and won't get me what I want. I became determined not to get caught in sharing my distorted version of "my truth." I studied people and figured out what they needed to know, what they wanted to hear, and who I needed to be to get what I wanted. My lies were much more believable and less bold in the creativity department. They were so reasonable that I believed them.

The likely stories eventually mixed with the absolute truth, and time became true over time by association. Like me being smart or a good singer, guitar player, actress, or student leader. I was those things. I let those absolute truths cover up deeper hidden untruths. I believed that what Mr. P did with me didn't affect me. That I was okay. I was okay. This habit was helpful as it helped me also slowly erase specific memories entirely as if they had never happened.

When I went to college, this selective memory served me well. If I believed it, it was easy to be believable. For the most part, it wasn't like I came to college with this made-up fantasy life to share—like the fact my dad owned a chocolate factory. It was more that my story evolved organically by points I simply chose to omit. I didn't share where I came from other than that I grew up in a town with two traffic lights, where one light blinked and the other changed colors. Truth.

Similarly, I'd share my high school successes—captain of cheerleading, a previous boyfriend whose family took me sailing on their boat to Martha's Vineyard, and how I dabbled in theatre and helped produce a closed-circuit morning news show at my high school. More truth. I'd carefully edit out details of those stories I didn't want others to know. It was storytelling by omission.

What they saw, I hoped, was a self-assured, smart, intelligent girl who worked hard and appeared a bit reserved but also knew how to have fun. Truth. I had all the accoutrements of a happy freshman: a boyfriend back home, matching comforter and shams, a stereo with an excellent record collection, clothes that were not homemade, and an amoeba-like personality that could naturally shift to the environment without even thinking about it.

I was invited to the dorm room across the hall from mine one night during freshman year. The "cool city girls'" room often smelled of pot and cigarettes. When their door opened, Rod Stewart or Van Halen blared from stereo speakers as girls from New York City and Long Island filtered out into the hallway. Those girls felt so worldly to me and, let's be honest, unattainable as potential friends.

Yet, when the offer came to hang with them, I nervously and eagerly accepted the invite. As I entered the room, I joined a circle of girls scattered on beds and the floor, sharing drinks in red Solo cups and snacks in brightly colored plastic bowls as "The Boss" blared from a turntable. This was a let's-get-to-know-each-other gathering. This was the real one—not the one our R.A. had in the lounge where she passed slips of papers with incomplete sentences we had to finish to get to know the other person in two minutes.

This was the college version of being picked for a team during high school gym class and praying with all your might that you would not be the last one standing.

I imagine I was on "high alert" when I entered the room, but it didn't show. I was used to watching and calculating my next move as if I were in a chess match.

Soon, we were all laughing and sharing bits about our high schools, hometowns, and majors. After more than a few Solo cup refills, the conversation shifted to the hot guys on campus, what activities and clubs we might join, and ultimately to any boyfriends we had back home.

Then the topic of virginity came up. We were building intimacy fast and furious. I remember thinking, *Well, I am a virgin*. They shared stories of planning elaborate "first time" special nights with their boyfriends before heading to college as they snuck into yachts floating on some dock in Long Island Sound or stealing the keys to the family vacation home in Connecticut after saying they were sleeping over at a friend's.

One girl shared a story of losing her virginity in the sweaty back seat of a car. *That one is real*, I remember thinking. I didn't say anything; I just absorbed what I was hearing, listening—always listening—and taking it all in. When their eyes turned to me, I smoothly and shyly confessed I was a virgin, cementing a persona that I and others were forming of me. I didn't even realize it was a lie.

Lying on my narrow bed later that night—and for many nights afterward—I started to question my virginity status for the first time. What is the truth? Wasn't I a virgin until it was my choice? Until I truly knew what I was doing and for love? What counted and what didn't? Did the expert hand or blow jobs I gave my boyfriend count? Did what Mr. P did to me—and made me do—matter? Where was the line?

Truth. It's sometimes hard to know where the absolute truth begins and ends. Truth can be messy. Truth can be salvation—but only when you own it.

Pequeño Mosquito

I ALWAYS WORKED. I BABYSAT MOST WEEKENDS OF MY HIGH SCHOOL YEARS. THE summer before I went to college and every summer during college, I needed to make enough money to help pay for school, which required me to hold three summer jobs simultaneously.

That summer, I started my day by 7 a.m. as a camp counselor, greeting the kiddos at the day camp in our town's summer recreation program. After pickup about eight hours later, I would hop in my car and head to my second and third jobs, either flipping burgers at Wendy's or waitressing in the beer garden at The Gelston House, a high-end restaurant overlooking the river closer to my home.

Often, I'd change my "uniform" from one job to the next in the backseat of my car.

I had to make enough money to go back to Marist. I was on a mission.

The Gelston House Beer Garden job paid the best and set the stage for one of my most dramatic public performances. It could have been a movie scene complete with background music building tension to a loud audience clap track.

Our customers docked their fancy boats to have a meal and a drink in the beer garden. Many of these uppity folks sporting—L.L. Bean, J. Crew, or Lacoste—became regulars, eventually requesting to be seated in my section. I often remembered their favorite drinks and ordered them from the bar as soon as they were seated in my section. They'd marvel at my memory and how I was such a nice girl working so hard. Some of my "regulars" took an interest in me, and a few tried to set me up with their snotty sons who could look down at me even as I stood taller before them while they sat at my table.

It didn't matter, as my bank account was filled by their generosity.

The summer between my freshman and sophomore years at Marist, despite not wanting to return to waitressing, I went back because I desperately needed the cash to make up the difference between what my scholarship offered and what Mom and Dad could no longer afford for tuition.

I had reservations about returning that summer because I had heard that the owner's son had taken over managing the beer garden, and he gave all of us the creeps. I had somehow survived that miserable summer with him in charge. It was early August, and I was counting down until my last shift. Just two more weeks, and I would have enough money for tuition.

It had been months of us grinning and bearing inappropriate comments from him, who had incidentally changed our uniform to one more appropriate for a current-day Hooters. I was sweaty and coming in and out of the kitchen that night as we had a line backed up at the hostess station. He commented about how sweaty I was and how he'd like to make me sweat. As if the comment wasn't enough, he touched my behind and gave it a squeeze.

Thanks to this type of behavior, we were short-staffed. The few of us who had stuck it out had had enough, including me.

I felt a rage I hadn't even known was there. That was it.

Turning toward him, I unsteadily set down my tray, ripped off my apron, and threw it at him. I did it. I quit amid the dinner rush while, much to my surprise, onlooking customers cheered and congratulated me!

Weeks later, before heading back to Marist, I called to arrange to pick up my last check. The day before I was to pick it up, Mom gave me an odd message: Someone called and told me the chef had requested my presence in his kitchen when I stopped in.

Puzzled, I decided the message must have gotten garbled. Chef, inviting *me* into the kitchen? This was quite an unusual and unsettling request.

If it were true, it filled me with a bit of terror. Was I in some trouble because of the way I quit? The kitchen was Chef's domain, and even as we servers entered to grab our orders from under the heat lamp, we never fully stepped into the full kitchen unless we had an excellent reason.

When I arrived at the appointed time the next day, the hostess pointed the way to the kitchen with a skeptical look. Once inside, Chef Espinoza—or Chef E—motioned me to sit at a small table beside the entrance. I waited, trying not to let him see how ruffled and anxious I was. Before I knew it, a fat, juicy, and expensive steak was spilling off the sides of a plate and in front of me. Covered with perfectly browned thin slices of onion and mushrooms and smothered in a rich gravy that pooled around the meat, it smelled heavenly.

With a smile revealing yellowed teeth, Chef sat across from me and urged me to eat it by waving his hands as if they were saying "ta-da!" He liked to call me his *pequeño mosquito* (small mosquito) because I was a tiny thing then—weighing less than 100 pounds—always buzzing in and out of the kitchen, especially during the dinner rush.

I know he probably knew—but ignored—those few times I had "accidentally" dropped one of the creamy, expensive, delicious cheesecakes the restaurant was known for while taking it out of the commercial refrigerator. We often had to bring the whole cheesecake from the big fridge to the prep area to be presliced so we could serve them quickly to drooling customers after dressing them with the fresh strawberries and crème fraîche the dessert chef had made. I had only dared to drop it once or twice because we had learned that if the cheesecake was flawed, the staff got to eat it. I was one of the few who dared to do it purposefully.

Thinking back to how Chef hunkered down in the chair, the soiled kitchen towel resting on his shoulder, slightly slumped over, watching me eat, I am sure this was his way of approving the dramatic end to my more-than-three-year waitress career. I ate gratefully and hungrily while he sat, satisfied and beaming.

Family

IMAGES THAT COME UP WHEN I HEAR THE WORDS "BROKEN HOMES" ARE GRAINY and emotional scenes of single working mothers struggling to do it all, divorced parents jostling kids between them, or worse yet—homes where drugs, alcohol, or abuse take its toll breaking the family bit by bit, day by day.

While both my parents were in the picture, and yes, we did struggle living close to and sometimes below the poverty level, and I experienced childhood trauma, I really never thought of us as being broken. Mom (and Dad) did the best they knew how. We were never without anything essential. Somehow, Mom made sure we had new school outfits, plenty of Christmas gifts under the tree, and a bit extra for an occasional treat. To this day, I have no idea how she did it.

It was just the life I knew. They were my family. We had plenty of laughs, joys, and challenges, but we were in it together.

Sure, when I was young, I fantasized about what it would be like to have a different family. You know, living in the well-kept two-story, two-car garage home surrounded by shrubs, trees, and a white picket fence. I'd wonder what it would be like to have a dad who left for "the office" every day carrying a briefcase. (Funny, he looked a lot like Darrin in *Bewitched*!) The mom in my vision—well, she was similar to my mom. Protective and resourceful, and obviously loved me—but maybe she was a better housewife, a bit more "put together," and didn't smoke so much.

I knew my parents loved me, but we didn't show it easily. It was more of an undercurrent that ran beneath it all. We weren't the touchy-feely family I craved. Ours wasn't the sit-on-my-lap-and-let-me-stroke-your-hair-and-hold-you kind of family. It was more hearing "Ya know I love ya, kid" a few times in my lifetime or having memories of the moments I felt my parents really saw me.

A few of those almost Hallmark moments are etched in my memory. That precious memory of Dad complimenting me as I appeared dressed for prom and telling me, "You are fucking beautiful," is one etched in my mind. It was one of the best compliments Dad could have given me. To me, it was equivalent with him saying he loved me.

I know love was there among the discarded car parts and the many challenges we faced as a family. We faced them together. We fiercely protected one another. Mom and Dad did their best, and I never felt I lacked anything essential. Sure, I envied the materialistic things my friends had or how effortless their lives seemed to move along in a perfectly planned trajectory while we painstakingly made it step by step.

From where I sit now, a sixty-plus-year-old woman who has raised three daughters and been married to my husband for over thirty-eight years, I wouldn't change a thing about my life. I know the white picket fence doesn't prevent bad stuff from happening anywhere.

At the risk of sharing an Oprah moment—what I know for sure is that I have a family of strong and loving siblings who have carved our own unique lives out of where we came from the best we could.

I'm proud of my family. Do I still wish I was closer to my siblings so I could be more a part of their lives and they in mine? Do I imagine the many ways I could have been more demonstrative with my love for my daughters? Holding them when they were little enough to let me and when they tried to wiggle away? Holding tighter just a bit longer? Do I struggle to share my love for my siblings even now? You bet.

Now that my daughters are carving their own lives in different cities, I wish I had hugged them more. I wish we had, even now, a "cuddle on the couch" relationship. But I know I couldn't have loved them any more than I do.

We all have to deal with our demons—with how things in our life landed on us and how to sort out all the messages we internalized despite their intended meaning.

Families vary. There is no one-size-fits-all, but as Dad might have said, "Families. They are fucking complicated, but you gotta love 'em, kid."

Love Lessons

have loved each other. It wasn't something I thought about much then, but I do now as an adult that has been married for more than half of her life.

As a teen, I came home too often to Mom, distraught at the kitchen table, chain-smoking and drinking coffee to dull whatever the source of the pain was that day. I am so grateful that my parents didn't reach for alcohol or something worse to absorb the pain of life's bumpy road.

One time, at age twelve, I sat down next to her as if I had wisdom to share. "Mom, you know you can leave Dad, don't you? You would be fine on your own. You could do it."

She lifted her head. Her face wore defeat, yet her eyes were clear. "You don't understand, Laurie. One day you will. Your dad and I belong together. We make it work."

She was right. I didn't understand. It would take me years of watching, living, and learning.

Struggle camouflaged their love. A love I couldn't see until years after they were gone. It was buried and overshadowed by the hardness of life. But it was there.

One lesson down; a few more to go.

With his shoulder-length blonde hair naturally wavy and bleached by the sun, Cody was beautiful. And at age sixteen, he was mine.

We were steady boyfriend and girlfriend in high school. Cody was one year older, yet we were a fixture from the moment we met. I'd faithfully attend his soccer games, and he'd watch me cheer from the sidelines of the field. I swear I could hear his applause over everyone else's after my music or theatre performances, and I saved rose petals from bouquets he gave me. (I still have them shriveled up in an old scrapbook.) We did homework together and took long drives—once Cody got his license— in his parent's car.

We went to my junior prom and his senior ball the same year. Mom had made my dress for junior prom, but I saved babysitting money for my slinky spaghetti strap number for senior ball. I still have a laminated picture of us—him tanned with a sparkling Crest smile aimed straight at the camera. We were quite a couple. Cody was wearing his white poly tux, oversized bow tie, and frilled shirt with edged stitching, an exact match to the shade of my lilac dress. In the photo, my Dorothy Hamill haircut was dressed up with a sprig of baby's breath, and Cody's arm was around me. We both stare straight at the camera, grinning self-satisfied Cheshire cat smiles. When I see my face now, I can see the mask I was so used to wearing.

I was fooling everyone but myself.

My parents weren't sure of Cody. Maybe they, too, thought he was too good to be true. That was until one night, hours after we had peeled out of my dirt driveway to attend a party, Cody brought me straight home. I was drunk. So drunk, he apologized to Mom and said something like, "I'm sorry, I didn't realize she'd get this drunk. I decided it would be better to bring her safely home."

Mom never said a word to me. She had her own method of punishment.

The following morning—as I sat curled by the toilet where I spent most of the night, she yelled for me all chirpy and cheery. She was never like this. "Laurie. Get up. I'm taking you to lunch and shopping! Just you and me!" She knew I felt horrible, but the last thing I'd do was let her know. She knew I'd rather suffer than admit how I felt and why.

We never spoke about it, but I learned my lesson. That was one of the longest days of my life.

I think that may have been the first time I was ever drunk. B.C. (before Cody) I didn't go to the popular crazy parties. I was invited occasionally but never really wanted to go. The parties where the popular gang hung out were more of my sister Maddy's thing. I often saw the popular kids sipping Boones Farm Strawberry Hill Wine from a shared bottle in the grocery store parking lot in the center of town. That kind of party did not appeal. Sure, I hung out with my friends, and we had our share of parties, but I had also shared plenty of my Saturday night dates with Dr. Pepper and a novel written by one of the Brontë sisters.

Mom and Dad let me take the car to spend weekends at UCONN with Cody when he was a freshman. The excitement of driving alone to "go away for the weekend to visit my boyfriend" quickly deflated once I realized I was "the high school girlfriend." I felt out of place and overwhelmed among the bouncy blonde college coeds attached to similarly striking boys. I had imagined walking along campus hand-in-hand. Having picnics on the quad and stealing kisses under a picturesque stone arch. Cody had other plans confined to his dorm room extra-long twin bed. Someone needing something from me. A familiar feeling. No longer feeling out of place, I complied.

Cody did come back to Higganum to attend my senior ball that year. Things felt different, and I needed to figure out why. After I graduated and was at Marist, the carefree and celebratory feel of that last summer must have fueled our relationship—along with letters we'd write and less-than-private hallway payphone calls that lasted as long as the coins in our pocket.

At Christmas break that first year back home, I knew things weren't working for us. But we were like a comfortable pair of well-worn socks we couldn't bear to be without.

We didn't know how to uncouple. Ironically enough, we lasted until Valentine's Day of my freshman year. I ended it dramatically by returning the medium-sized Russell Stover cardboard heart of chocolates he had sent me after many missed calls, weeks without letters, and me feeling abandoned. I took his most likely hastily purchased pharmacy candy out of the package, ripped the red envelope inside without opening it, stomped on the heart of chocolates, put it all back in the padded envelope, and sent it back "Return to Sender."

Being Cody's girlfriend for those many years were my training wheels for love and life. It was like we were playing house. We'd pretend. I was on familiar ground when I was pretending.

When I was a kid, I loved playing house. Jack, Maddy, and I would sneak Mom's broom out back in the woods and sweep the ground underneath a tree so much it was hard and felt like a shiny kitchen floor. We'd mark out the house. This section here, behind the tree trunk, was the bedroom. This area here, marked by the big rock, was the kitchen. Once the house was ready, we'd play-act what ordinary families might do. What we saw on TV. You know, the ones where the dad comes home from work with a briefcase, and the mom greets him at the door with dinner ready, and they talk about the day before the kids come to the table.

Cody and his family allowed me to step into that kind of life and see it act out in real time.

They had a blacktop drive that led up a hill to an attached garage framed by neatly trimmed bushes and symmetrically arranged flowers. Cody's mom offered homemade snacks after school—cookies or brownies warm from the oven and a glass of cold milk. They all ate dinner together, waiting until after his dad had a chance to "unwind" with a drink in his study after coming home from work. They had two tables to eat on: one shiny Formica in the kitchen surrounded by bright windows facing a garden and another fancy wooden one with legs like a dancer's gracefully curving toward the oriental rug on the dining room floor.

I observed and absorbed. This was where I learned which fork to use and witnessed how a typical family operated. I saw a husband and wife with a different kind of love than at home. I now know it wasn't necessarily better, but it gave me something to shoot for back then.

His family accepted me for who they saw in front of them—their son's polite, friendly girlfriend. They didn't ask too many questions about my family. I don't think they wanted to know.

Of course, his family owned a sailboat they kept at a dock on the shore a short drive from Higganum. Some weekends, I would tag along, help sand dried algae off the hull, and do whatever was needed to prepare the boat for the water. In the summer—and sometimes on crisp early fall weekends—they would include me on a sail around Long Island Sound or an overnight trip to Block Island.

I loved being with them. No longer anchored to my life, I was along for the ride in theirs. Feeling free, open to possibility. Feeling what I thought normal must feel like. Being a part of something, even for a brief time.

Cody and I would sneak down to the marina some nights. Our bodies in a heightened state of anticipation. Adrenaline flowing. It felt exciting. We knew we were doing something we shouldn't or thinking about what we really wanted to do. In the dark below deck, with the boat swaying, the wire side stays banging against the mast in the wind; I learned a little bit more about love and sex. I felt like I was someone else with Cody.

I didn't know what was expected when it came to making out as a teen. What I knew about sex was confusing. I didn't even know it was sex. Like most teenage girls, we whispered about what guys wanted at slumber parties. How it might feel. How guys just wanted to get girls to "home base." I played along. I didn't realize what I knew wasn't even in the game. That my model for intimacy was perverted and twisted.

Cody wanted to be my first. He could never be.

In college, though, I fell in love.

No. That's not it. I dove straight off the cliff headfirst into love. Into lust. Into him.

I was overtaken by some unseen force pulling me to him. It scared and thrilled me simultaneously. The image of us together gripped me, holding me so tight that I wanted to be with him more than anything. The thought of him suffocated me, and I couldn't breathe in his presence.

What was happening to me? This fully buttoned up and in control girl who was always two steps ahead—never out of control—was whirling like a leaf in a wind tunnel.

Was this love? I was confused. I didn't realize what it was. And I didn't care.

Bill was my first encounter with desire. Pure animalistic lust.

Perhaps the internal automatic need radar I had developed that faithfully alerted me whenever anyone wanting or needing came within a close radius was backfiring. That feeling was like a kneading energy I despised. My self-developed warning system had served me well for years. It kept me safe as I was repulsed by others' need of me, yet here I was, helpless with need for him. Bill was perfect for me. He didn't need me, rendering my internal warning system useless.

I couldn't get enough of the wanting. Me wanting to be with him. To smell him. To see his smile and feel his touch. Oh, God. I even wanted to feel him naked beside me. What??? Really Laurie?

Was I becoming the animal Mr. P was?

What was happening to me?

Bill entered my life via the crew team. It was the one place I felt the most control until he entered the picture.

He wasn't in my boat, but I noticed him well before he noticed me.

I'd see him in the tanks and the gym and walking across campus. Usually alone, he was quiet and mysterious. I watched him. What I saw I liked. Very much.

He was purposeful. Reserved. Unique. He was an enigma—even after we started dating.

He wore vintage and second-hand clothes well before they were fashionable. He had style. Shirts, ironed and crisp. He was buttoned up. He seldom spoke. The words he did utter were chosen carefully. Dark hair cut short—unlike most guys on campus, letting their hair grow loose and long.

We started being friends by talking about music. New music from the U.K. Robert Smith and The Cure. Psychedelic Furs. Import albums you could only get if you ordered them at the record store in the Poughkeepsie downtown mall. Depeche Mode. Ramones.

Even after we started being a couple, I was never sure he liked me. My desire for him overshadowed my need for him to like me. I convinced myself it didn't matter. I didn't care. As long as I could be with him.

Despite how controlled Bill appeared, it was he who taught me to let go—even just a little. I decided that he was my real first.

He helped me explore my body and what it could feel. I remember lying hot and sweaty in his bed, him reaching for an ice cube from the glass on the nightstand, and how my body reacted. He slowly ran the melting ice cube down the front of my body. My body quivered and twitched—as he reached lower and lower. My mind never stood a chance.

This was unfamiliar, and oh so. . .so. . .amazing.

And the release.

I cried. I was embarrassed. He kissed my tears away.

Bill awakened a part of me I hadn't known was there. He was my drug. Our tumultuous relationship ignited something deep inside me that I'd spend my entire life working hard to keep lit.

We were on again, off again a few years after college. I was heartbroken when we were no longer together. It took me years to decouple from him emotionally. I was afraid if I let him go, the sleeping sexual desire in me he had awakened would go, too.

For the last thirty-eight years, I've learned a lot about love—a deeper, committed kind of care, respect, and trust that I never knew existed.

As Rich and I age, we often look at each other and marvel with gracious gratitude how we have played a critical role in healing our childhood wounds together.

We fit together like puzzle pieces—sometimes. Our children often remind us that we also lash out and clash but quickly return to an equilibrium of respect and gratitude.

Love is push-and-pull, give-and-take, but with grace and kindness as its guide.

Our love allowed me to find myself. It filled holes that I wasn't sure how to fill—or never believed could be filled. It allowed me the safety to risk standing on the razor's edge of pain and hurt—to be present with it, explore it, understand it, and ultimately leap into it, trusting I'd survive the fall.

With Rich's love, I survived. My sense of self grew with it. With Rich's support, patience, and willingness to walk with me—holding me tight as we navigated the dark tunnel of healing my childhood sexual wounds—I not only survived. I began to thrive.

It wasn't easy, and I never thought it was possible, but I can claim with conviction that I know so much more about love now than I ever thought possible. How to love myself enough to know what I need and want and ask for it in the moment I want and need it? How to give of myself without feeling it's part of a deal I am making, expecting something in return?

The love lessons my committed relationship with Rich have taught me are as precious and unfortunately as rare as a colored diamond. I have learned to listen to my body—know who I am—and allow that person to show up in the world, unapologetic and without the need to pretend.

Writing this book is a big part of this.

I am owning my truth with all its messiness so that I can claim this life that I have had without regret and with gratitude.

I'm unsure if love makes the world go around, but it helps us become whole. The power it holds can heal even the deepest pain. I know that. I, with Rich's support and love, can now let down my defenses, be vulnerable, and show my underbelly, I gained the gifts of what it is like to truly be seen, accepted, and loved for all I am.

There is no greater gift.

It is something worth striving for. It is life's greatest love lesson.

Unexpected Gifts

HE WAS ALWAYS IN MY LIFE. I DON'T REMEMBER A TIME WITHOUT HIS PRESENCE in the shadows.

His dark form appears in the periphery of so many family Polaroid snapshots.

There he is—standing in the corner, drink in hand—looming over us kids as we sat in PJs, scattered around the Christmas tree, ripping the wrapping off our gifts. He's seated, gussied up in a nice shirt but no tie, feasting on turkey with the fixin's at almost all of the Thanksgivings I can remember. Waving to me as I peeked out the back window of the car as my parents drove me to college. Mr. P was present—in the background—at whatever birthday parties we hosted, surrounded by childhood classmates, friends, and neighbor children whose parents had unknowingly dropped their kids off to be within reach of a pedophile. He was in the background at milestone events—graduations and, yes, in a tux at my wedding.

Shadow is a good word for him. Because shadows need light to exist.

Our relationship was not all dark. Throughout the years, many bright moments have brought me happiness and joy. It is complex. Mr. P was often the source of much-needed attention. I felt cared for by him in a weird sort of way. I felt special—as every human being needs to feel.

Despite the cost that I wasn't aware I was paying—he did take away the feeling that I was a piece of junk. There were many moments he made me feel that I was—well—wanted—because, quite simply, that was the ugly truth. Wanting was a big part of our relationship.

A teeter-totter of want.

Mr. P did want and need me. It just wasn't in the way we all wish for. Unfortunately, I needed him, too.

As I write those words, my stomach tightens, and I feel sick. What a way to get that baseline human need met. I grieve for "little Laurie." She didn't know any better. But he did.

While he did choose me to be his victim, I did my best not to feel like one.

My brain did what brains do.

Wired for survival—neurons formed connections with other neurons via synapses creating superhighways of learned behavior and thought patterns. I created and cultivated beliefs that enabled me to shift and dull the pain and terrifying moments, so I wouldn't easily "remember" those intense memories.

I had a lot of practice pushing those dark bits back into the recesses—into the shadow of my mind. My developing brain rerouted the circuitry so I wouldn't suffer for long. I trained myself to focus on whatever light I could find. Like an insect, I was attracted to and sought out any source of light I could.

Perhaps that's why I gravitated to the bright lights of the stage in middle school, high school, and college. This may be why the power of pretend took hold of me.

Seek the light. Seek the light. My brain must have kept that on repeat.

I was the unfortunate seed lodged in the dark and deep recess of a hairline sidewalk crack. I became the seedling struggling to push its way up through the concrete toward what it needed to grow and survive.

Dwarfed by lack of light, I twisted this way and that way for years—seeking any source of the sun's warmth—so I could live and survive. I said and believed whatever I needed to. This habit allowed me not just to survive but thrive.

Today, if you ask my family or any of my friends, work colleagues, or clients—they would say I am an eternal optimist. The mindful Buddha seeks the gifts in whatever is there. Acceptance leaves my glass always half full. I live for the light.

During therapy, I learned that not all victims of sexual abuse come out of their situations as I have.

I'm not pretending all is perfectly fine. You can ask my husband, Rich, how hard we've worked on intimacy. Ask my kids about my insane instinctual need to protect them so they never feel pain or disappointment. My compulsion to find the bits we can "control" in life so there are no surprises, no cliffs to fall off of.

Yes, the shadows still trip me up.

I somehow turned my attraction to the light into one of my "superpowers." It's served me well.

I embrace the yin-yang of life. Good-bad, sweet-sour, dark-light— one can't exist without the other.

While I can never forgive Mr. P for how much pain and suffering he caused me, shining light on all of those experiences has allowed me to uncover many gifts in my life. For that, I am thankful.

It's taken most of my adult life to recognize how broken and damaged Mr. P was to want and need me in the way he did. It wasn't right. It was so very wrong.

Yet, I choose to forgive him.

And to forgive him, I must thank *me*!

I am so very grateful to whatever was inside me that fought for that light despite the darkness Mr. P pushed me into.

The compassionate heart I have today is the result of many lessons Mr. P taught "little Laurie" so early in life, lessons I may not have learned without those experiences. Lessons that have helped me become the woman I am today. Lessons that give me the gift of appreciating it all—the messiness of life, the light, and yes, the dark too.

I certainly don't thank Mr. P for what he did to me, but I can forgive him for it, and I do.

Because of him I have learned how to choose to shift shadows into the light so I can shine.

Shine, Laurie. Shine.

Whirrip. . .
Whirrip. . .Whirrip

I'VE BEEN TOLD THAT THE MOST STRESSFUL LIFE EVENTS ARE THE DEATH OF A loved one, divorce (or marriage), moving, a significant injury or illness, and job loss. Perhaps it was cinematic kismet or life once again, seeing just how much I could handle when, in late summer or early fall of 1987, Rich and I experienced many of these life events simultaneously.

Rich and I had taken new jobs in Boston. He was transitioning to a sales and marketing job for IBM, and I took a job at a public relations firm. We had purchased a lovely two-story home with a sloped yard in historic Wakefield, Massachusetts, on the North Shore and were settling in nicely.

We accepted an offer on our Poughkeepsie duplex when we learned we had to evict our tenant to close. This was no small feat, requiring multiple trips for hearings and trying to work things out with the tenant who had owed us back rent for the past four months. While we didn't expect to get paid for the back rent, we just needed the tenant to move so we could close. Rich traveled back and forth to Poughkeepsie, juggling the training demands of his new job, and in the end, with no other option, he ended up driving there days before our wedding to meet the Dutchess County Sheriff to move her things out into the street. It was awful.

Those months were crazy busy—we had made the move to Boston after purchasing a new home, started new jobs, tried to sell our Poughkeepsie duplex, and planned our wedding just weeks away.

Then, Mom's illness took a turn for the worse.

We had been here before—many times. I had gotten calls intermittently as a Marist student and then for years afterward. Each time, no matter where I was, I would get in the car and drive to the hospital, wondering if it would be my last trip to stand by her bedside. 'all were tired by this point, so wasn't she? Mom had been fighting her emphysema diagnosis for almost five years. Fighting with each breath she struggled to take.

She had even been admitted to the ICU, where hospital priests blessed her with her last rights—more than once. I'd often wondered if that made Mom especially blessed and, each time it happened, if this time it truly would be her actual last rights.

She recently came out of what had been a semi-coma state, surprising her doctors once again. I think Ryan or Cindy told me that the hospital staff were calling her "the miracle lady" since they had no idea how her body continued to function given the advanced stage of her emphysema. By this point, her lungs were pumping less than 30 percent of the oxygen her body needed, and they had never seen a body continuing to keep going when oxygen levels were so much less than what organs required to function. It was a miracle.

We had all hoped that if we emphasized significant family milestones and life events, Mom would have something to look forward to and keep going. It worked.

First, Cindy was pregnant with her first child. Mom glowed more and more as Cindy's belly grew. When Cindy and James, my brother-in-law and her second husband, gave birth to chubby-cheeked Noah, we all felt the lift, but Mom especially. Mom loved him so much, and we saw the color come back into her skin and her eyes brighten as she embraced her role as Grandma. Then, Rich proposed to me, and we had something else to look forward to. Mom buoyed again as we planned my wedding and looked forward to being there for the big day.

In the weeks before the wedding, while Rich drove to Poughkeepsie to (hopefully) close on the duplex, I ran back and forth to Connecticut, finalizing the wedding details and keeping tabs on Mom's declining health.

With just a few days until our big day, my nose was hit by the strong smell of disinfectant as soon as I stepped out of a hospital elevator clutching the visitor's pass. I walked, looking down at the worn linoleum floor as I approached the nurses' station to ask for further directions to Mom's room.

My mind raced as I walked down the hallway toward her room.

I'm glad she is out of the ICU. Does this mean she will be able to attend the wedding? We should cancel. That's the right thing to do. What if we don't, and she actually— Oh, god, I can't think about that. Don't think about that. Where is she?

I pushed the slightly ajar door to find Mom sleeping while a machine beside her breathed for her. I sighed, and although the sound was loud, its cadence somehow soothed me.

Whirrip. . .whirrip. . .whirrip.

I pulled a plastic chair beside her bed and sank into it, trying not to notice the noisy apparatus and machinery surrounding her. I traced a few of the plastic tubes coming from some of the machines. They snaked around the bed, some extra tubing coiled near the floor ultimately attached to the mask covering her mouth and nose. I noticed bruising where the IV went into her arm. I wondered if it was hurting her. If she knew I was there.

As she struggled to breathe, so did I.

Whirrip. . .whirrip. . .whirrip.

My heart was heavy with so many thoughts and wishes.

Whirrip. . .whirrip. . .whirrip.

After seeing Mom struggle for so long—we were all tired of the fight.

Was she ready to give up now? Was this the day?

Whirrip. . .whirrip. . .whirrip.

Too many thoughts were tearing me in two. I wanted relief for her. And I so desperately wanted her to be there to see me walk down the aisle wearing the vintage wedding dress that the seamstress had to keep taking in more and more as we got closer to the wedding. *Were my nerves shrinking me?*

Whirrip. . .whirrip. . .whirrip.

Mom, I just want you to see I am—I will be okay. All I want is one more memory with you—to have you and Dad share in this moment with us. Given all you've lived through, is that too much to ask? I want you to see I am building a good life with Rich.

Whirrip. . .whirrip. . .whirrip.

The thoughts and emotions continued to teeter-totter—swinging to and fro. Afraid I would wake her, I tried to sit up but stuck to the chair a bit. I sat back down, breathing and looking at her. Her skin looked translucent and gray, but I was used to that as if she wasn't getting enough oxygen; that would often happen. She looked tired. Suddenly my thoughts were interrupted by a nurse briskly brushing by me to check the machines. She smiled at me and woke Mom to check her temperature and record some vitals on the chart hanging at the foot of her bed.

Whirrip. . .whirrip. . .whirrip.

Mom looked up and saw me as a faint smile appeared from behind the oxygen mask. I was used to looking at her from behind the plastic paraphernalia. We looked into each other's eyes, recognizing the pain we each saw.

Whirrip. . .whirrip. . .whirrip.

Maybe she was wondering if she'd make it to the wedding too. Or perhaps she was trying to envision what I'd look like as a bride. Maybe both.

Whirrip. . .whirrip. . .whirrip.

I felt a tear roll down my cheek and the sting of my next thought.

Whirrip. . .whirrip. . .whirrip.

Not daring to say it aloud, I thought, *Mom, why am I just starting to live my life when you are getting ready to end yours?*

I hovered over her, my tears making wet spots on the bleached blue dotted pattern on her hospital gown as I took her gray hand in mine, and we continued to look at each other wordlessly.

Whirrip. . .whirrip. . .whirrip.

Please. Stop.

Whirrip. . .whirrip. . .whirrip.

No. Don't stop.

Whirrip. . .whirrip. . .whirrip.

Mom's eyes slowly closed as if they could no longer focus or remain open.

Whirrip. . .whirrip. . .whirrip.

I sat there. With her. Holding and stroking, the thin skin stretched over her plump fingers, the result of her body retaining water.

I just wanted time to stop. To be with her without thinking about the future. So that's what I did.

Whirrip. . .whirrip. . .whirrip.

Miracles

MY EYES SLOWLY OPEN, AND FOR A FEW SECONDS, I AM GROGGY, DISORIENTED, and unsure of where I am. Then, in an instant, it hits me as a rush of chemicals causes me to sit straight upright in my twin bed. My eyes widen as I take in familiar surroundings. There is the old dresser where the drawers stick so much you have to tug until they jerk open. The no-longer white eyelet runner is stained, crooked, and wrinkled, still supporting a collection of rocks, assorted square cardboard jewelry boxes, Grandma's old perfume bottles, and dusty Hummel figurines given to me for significant life events like communion and my high school graduation.

I pull up the covers and snuggle up. I know where I am and why as my eyes land on my dress hanging on the edge of the closet door. I take in the translucent layers of antique silk, and my heart fills. It is September 19, 1987, and I'm getting married today!

A few hours later, everyone is here, buzzing around. Maddy, Cindy, and Jack are all here. Ryan was sent out on wedding errands while Mr. P, Dad, and Mom sat around our old round kitchen table drinking coffee.

MOM IS HERE! I felt like shouting. Yet, I had promised myself I'd be relaxed and casual on the outside despite my fear that the day would be too much for her. Less than a week ago, we had no idea she would still be with us. Rich and I had talked to Dad about contingency plans, just in case.

Yet, here she was, after a week or two of Mom negotiating mini-miracle milestones with her doctors so she could be released from the hospital in time to attend the wedding.

Shortly after my visit a few weeks prior, she had been discharged from the ICU to a regular hospital room. Unfortunately, it wasn't looking too good. Her doctors had no idea how her heart and other organs were still functioning, given that they had been oxygen-deprived for so long.

Yet, Mom had a reputation as "the miracle lady," often pulling through what should have been fatal health scares. A few times, she had rolled out of the hospital in a wheelchair weeks after the hospital priest administered "last rites." Once Mom got something in her head, there was no talking her out of it.

A few days after getting sprung from the ICU, Dad said that Mom, still attached to numerous monitors, weakly asked one of her doctors if he thought she could attend her daughter's wedding in a few weeks.

Dad said the doc skeptically told her they could talk about it if she could sit in bed the next day. Sure enough, Mom was sitting up the next day when her doctor entered her room. So she asked again, and he told her, "If tomorrow you can eat something. . ." and then. . . "If you can swing your legs to the side of the bed. . ." and then . . . "If you can walk to the bathroom. . ." until a few days ago, Dad picked her up and brought her home so she could be with us.

Hallelujah! Another miracle recovery thanks to Mom's strong will and stoic stubbornness.

So here she was. Gasping to catch her breath despite sitting in the wheelchair and hooked up to her oxygen machine, plastic tubes securely fashioned to her nostrils with tape.

She was here for me.

My maid of honor, Ellie, a true friend I had made late in high school and kept in touch with during college, was also buzzing around, helping us get ready before the photographer arrived. Then, finally, Ryan came in carrying a large cardboard box he had picked up from the florist. My heart was pounding with excitement as we opened it.

Having done more of the wedding planning via mail and phone, I had sent the florist carefully curated *Bride* magazine photos of what I wanted for all the bouquets. Carefully unwrapping them from layers of waxy green paper, I was pleased. They looked just as I had pictured them.

I rummaged through the box, seeking the simple, delicate crown of flowers I had asked them to create for me. I had shipped them a clear plastic comb with rhinestones to weave into the crown so it would easily attach to my veil and not shift while dancing. I had agonized over how it should look, sending them several photos with red ink circles indicating those that were too full that I didn't want, and others I had wildly circled in purple ink indicating the crowns on the page I loved and wanted.

My face fell and my heart rate rose as I pulled out a bulbous circle headpiece crammed full of carnations (the big ones, not the minis I had suggested) and ferny, spiky green things shooting out in all directions. It looked exactly like the ones I had circled with red ink that I hated.

"Oh my," Ellie exclaimed, exchanging knowing looks with me since she and I had debated and discussed how a simple floral headpiece would be just the right touch with the fifties-style silk organza wedding dress I had scored from a local antique store for the unbelievable price of 125 dollars.

Determined not to let anything ruin my day, I took a deep breath and pulled out the carnations and the ferns until they were sparse. Mom was shrieking, "Laurie, what are you doing?" Head down and focused, we ignored her pleas to stop, until, after adding a few sprigs of baby's breath we had gently extracted from the bouquets, I stepped back and realized it would do!

The photographer snapped photos of all of us in multiple combinations. Me, gazing wistfully into a mirror in my parent's bedroom. Ellie, pretending to straighten my veil. My sisters, fixing my hair. All the required prewedding poses I had imagined my album would include.

Mr. P wasn't in the wedding party but was there since he now lived in a trailer on our property. Dad had let him put it just down the hill and into the woods near where our new house was built after he had sold the junkyard below. Mr. P was wearing a suit. I didn't even know he owned one. At one point, he asked the photographer to take a photo with me. We stood stiffly next to one another as the photographer quickly snapped, and we moved on to the next shot.

I was happy. Possibly the happiest I had ever felt in our house.

At one point, the photographer, noticing Mom was out of breath, sat her in our most comfortable chair. He anticipated that I might not want to look back at photos of her in her wheelchair. He directed me to stand behind her. I rested my arms around her neck and leaned in to kiss the top of her head before he snapped the photo. She smelled just like Mom. I relaxed into her a bit. I felt her strong shoulders going up and down as she tried to catch her breath. I wanted so badly to lessen her load. I wanted to take care of her. The thought crossed my mind that with a husband at my side, I could.

Despite her grayish pallor, Mom was radiant in the loosely fitting mauve dress Cindy had selected for her while she had been in the hospital. For the next photo, Maddy, Cindy, and Ellie joined in, surrounding Mom and me, their pink taffeta bridesmaid dresses with the large bows in the back, just as the Butterick pattern had indicated.

It was happening. I was getting married to Rich.

Mom was here. She made it.

Hours later, after dodging pouring rain, I was in the church's vestibule in Middletown, Connecticut, with Dad and my bridesmaids. Ellie, Cindy, Maddy, and my three soon-to-be sisters-in-law surrounded me in a cloud of pink. Rich nervously awaited me at the altar with his groomsmen, Ryan, Jack, and some of his best buddies from high school and college—Dave, R. Steven, and his best man and cousin, John.

Early in our planning, Rich and I realized that despite always dreaming of getting married in our precious little St. James Church in Higganum, the parish I grew up in and where Mom had served on church council all those years was too small to hold our guest list. The current St. James reverend had arranged for us to get married in a larger Episcopalian church in Middletown, much closer to the Marriott Hotel, where we were having the reception.

Just before the music began, signaling the girls to walk up the aisle toward Rich and his groomsmen, Jack suddenly appeared at my side with a sweet grin and a small velvet box. His sweet face shone with adorableness, and he may have even been teary-eyed as he whispered to me, "This is from Rich. He wanted you to have this. He wants you to feel like a princess, Laurie."

I opened the box to see a beautiful pearl ring surrounded by diamonds. It was the exact ring I had seen when we purchased our wedding rings at the small family-owned store in the Boston jewelry district. When I saw it in the case, I timidly asked the clerk if I could try it on, but upon seeing the price tag, I eventually selected another one with smaller diamonds that fit my engagement ring better.

Rich had secretly bought it anyway. I had two rings! As I slipped the pearl and diamond ring on my right ring finger, I felt something I'd never felt. It was more than feeling loved by Rich; it was the feeling of being cherished and worthy of love.

Like Rich and I, the ring slipped on with ease and fit perfectly.

I walked down the aisle with Dad, a beaming princess. Then, less than an hour later, I walked back down with Rich, a radiant wife.

Mom stayed for most of the reception, her oxygen tank taking up the seat beside her. She had made it to my wedding against all odds.

She died at the age of fifty-seven, just three months later. But she had made it to my wedding.

A Mountain of Dreams

IN 1988, LESS THAN A YEAR AFTER MOM PASSED AWAY, DAD SOLD THE PRE-FAB house on top of Watson Hill and left the junkyard behind. He bought an old farmhouse on "half a mountain" in Cambridge, New York. Dad had always dreamed of living on and owning his own mountain.

Rich and I had spent many weekends visiting to help him refurbish it. Together, we made much-needed updates to the house, smashing old lathe and plaster walls that were already falling apart and replacing them with new drywall. Sanding, painting, and refinishing floors. We helped clear some old farmland that hadn't been used in quite a while so Dad could have a small vegetable garden. Dad loved the land, and I'd never seen that part of him.

I didn't know then that time spent with him would be so precious.

We were at the farm one hot July day on his sixtieth birthday. Rich and I were teasing him that he was an old man now. He shot up from the picnic table and said, "Fuck no; I'll show you I'm not."

Within minutes, he started to climb a tree and wouldn't come down! He sat up on a branch in his dingy "white" V-neck t-shirt, looking child-like as his legs dangled from the branch above our heads. He sat up there for quite some time, enjoying the view from that vantage point, taking in the acreage that stretched out around him that he owned. We let him sit there, enjoying the lovely view of his land.

When he finally came down, with the aid of a stepladder and some insistence from us that he "go slow," he and Rich began to work on roto-tilling the garden. Before long, an argument ensued about the proper way to do it. Before anger could spoil the moment, Rich grabbed the nearby wheelbarrow we had given him as a gift and told Dad to hop in. Dad did, and Rich pushed Dad around the yard. What had been a tense moment shifted as we all began to laugh at how Dad looked being pushed around in the wheelbarrow. I hadn't seen Dad smile or laugh like that in such a long time. It felt good to be joyful together. I felt something loosen up in all of us. Things felt free.

We continued visiting Dad as often as possible, using various house projects as an excuse. With each visit, it seemed Dad was getting older and more ornery than I had ever thought possible.

One afternoon, Rich was getting impatient, waiting for Dad to wake up so they could take out a wall in the living room. Rich tried to wake him one too many times, and while I was in the kitchen making lunch, I heard the sound of the chainsaw before I saw Dad in his sagging BVD underwear, chasing Rich, threatening to cut off a part of his anatomy that I shall not mention!

Rich ran outside and didn't return for an hour, giving Dad time to settle down.

Dad stayed up so much later than we could and then slept in—often into the late afternoon. It began to feel like we hardly saw him all weekend. I could sense our time together getting shorter, especially as I noticed a shortness of breath—the sound of his rasping eerily reminiscent.

One day in fall 1989, shortly after we arrived for another weekend visit, Dad, Rich, and I sat at his small kitchen table, and he told us he was sick. His salt and pepper hair slicked back on his head as it hung low, cigarette still burning in the ashtray beside his coffee cup; he told us he had lung cancer. He said it was too late to do much about it and hoped it would be much quicker than Mom.

Dad had a few bouts of chemotherapy, but he told us he didn't want to die feeling like that. While we wanted him to live, we knew deep inside we couldn't watch him die slowly like Mom had. We didn't have that in us.

Dad had always been interested in new age topics, including the occult, reincarnation, spiritual energy consciousness, and alternative healing modalities. He reluctantly continued with chemo and turned his hope to Barbara Brennan, a world-renowned healer. He had read several of her books. She was a former NASA physicist who had developed energetic healing techniques based on science. She promoted a healing protocol that promised to help clear, balance, and renew our energy fields to promote self-healing.

We contacted her newly formed Barbara Brennan School of Healing, securing him a few healing appointments with Barbara herself!

The sessions gave Dad hope, but even he admitted it was too late.

Our visits to the farm became more frequent as Dad became weaker. He entered hospice in December 1989.

Rich and I were attending our friends Jean and Steve's wedding in the Hudson Valley of New York on December 30, 1989. Knowing we were not far from Dad, we called on New Year's Eve to check in and tell him we'd be stopping by. It was then we learned from his caregiver that Dad had taken a turn for the worse and had been admitted to Albany VA Hospital. We needed to get there as soon as possible!

We raced to the Albany VA Hospital. My body auto-reacted to the hospital smells and sounds. Upon entering Dad's room, I found myself leaning on Rich to keep me upright. It was all too familiar. Instead of Mom, here was Dad. He looked worn out. Old. So very small.

My insides tightened.

After getting an update from the friendly and supportive hospice staff and realizing Dad's systems were shutting down, we knew we had to gather the family. We were given access to a small private living room outside Dad's. Using the phone there, I started making phone calls, trying desperately to reach everyone on New Year's Eve. It took some doing, but I got a hold of my sister Cindy, who helped us reach everyone else.

Rich and I spent time with Dad while we waited for everyone to drive to Albany. I sat there, holding his hands in mine, wondering when I last touched him so lovingly. I felt a sting of shame when I realized I couldn't remember.

Sitting there, I stared at his face for a long time. I talked to him. Telling him everyone was on their way.

Dad looked vulnerable and serene. He seemed to be softening before my eyes.

For all of Dad's rough and tough exterior, he was always a sensitive man deep inside. Dad was like one of my favorite childhood penny candies—a fireball. The first few minutes of it were pure hell, setting your mouth on fire in seconds. You just had to wait for it, and you'd reach the sweet cinnamon center—well worth the pain to get there. A relationship with Dad was like that. Eventually, you'd endure some pain to get to the softer, sweeter side.

I sat there enjoying this bittersweet moment.

Within a few hours, everyone started to arrive, and eventually, we all made it while Dad was going in and out of consciousness. The nurses assured us he wasn't feeling any pain. He would lie there relaxed and peaceful, only to awaken suddenly, eyes open, confused, and in the moment with us. He drifted back and forth in this manner. We imagined his spirit moving from in and out of his body as he had often told us happened when someone was dying.

A few weeks before this, Dad had said he was "done" with dying and just wanted to find out once and for all if what the sheiks and mystics claimed was true. "I guess one good thing about dying is that I'll finally see for myself what the big deal is about the afterlife," he had said.

Dad had always believed in reincarnation and that our souls live on after our "body suits" die. He told Rich that upon his death, he would send us a sign that he was right. He said while he didn't know what type of things he'd still be able to do when he was no longer on "this earthly plane," he'd do his best to do something. He wanted to tell us if all this "shit was made up or was real." He then added he sure hoped that there was indeed a beautiful, peaceful place beyond death because if this was the total end, "it wasn't fucking worth it."

We all gathered around Dad that first night of 1990 after we had each taken turns having a private moment with him to say our goodbyes. We had given him permission to let go. We told him we would all be okay. That we appreciated how hard life had been, and it was now time for him to go.

As if we scripted it, his eyes opened up, and you could see the clarity in his eyes. He was there with us. He whispered to us, "It's like I said. It's beautiful. More than you can ever imagine. So beautiful." Sighing, he closed his eyes. Watching his face and body closely, we all held our breath. Waiting. And then, Dad opened his eyes and said, "Don't worry. I'll send you a sign. I promise."

Silence fell in the room, and we exchanged tearful yet hopeful looks. We all had hoped that what Dad believed and was experiencing was as serene and beautiful as he had said.

Shortly afterward, the nurse came in and suggested we all take a break so they could make Dad a bit more comfortable. We gathered in the small room next to Dad's. Someone mentioned it was past midnight, and at least Dad had made it to a new decade.

A few minutes later, the nurse told us Dad had passed.

The Junkyard Shaman's body was gone, as was the difficulty of his life. The image that he was now up to his crazy shenanigans in some beautiful place comforted me.

A few weeks later, Rich and I went to the farmhouse to gather a few of Dad's things. Dad had one of those touch lights at his bedside. You simply had to touch it slightly to turn it on.

While we were looking for a few things in his bedroom, the light flickered. We both looked at each other without surprise. Then it blinked again as if to say, "I told you so." I whispered to the stale air in the room, "Thanks, Dad, for letting us know. Glad you are okay."

Before we got into the car to head home, I took a good look at his land and the mountain behind his house. I felt Dad there among the trees and the mountaintop. He was finally free.

Broken Silence—Part 1

I WAS SOMETIMES THE STAIRWAY SENTRY. SOMEONE HAD TO BE ON THE LOOKOUT.

It happened regularly. Mom would get pissed at our bickering and send us all to our room. I say our room because when we were young, all three of us—me, Maddy, and Jack—shared a room and a bed.

I don't remember when, but at some point, Mom and Dad must have realized it wasn't good for Jack to still be with us girls. He ended up moving to the large room to the right of the stairs—literally steps from ours—to sleep in Mr. P's room.

Yes. Jack was moved to Mr. P's room.

Just writing that sentence feels like a punch in the gut. Little Jack living in the same room as that monster. Well, he did get to have a TV in his room. At least he got that. Yet, he had gotten so much more than we all had thought.

At my age, I didn't know what a pedophile was—let alone one who might like both girls and boys. I wouldn't honestly know the impact Mr. P had on our entire family for at least another thirty years or so when, in my forties and at the encouragement of my therapist, I set up a family meeting at a motel in Connecticut to have a "chat" about Mr. P and what I was remembering.

I needed help sorting out the confusing scenes I was beginning to remember and convincing myself I had made up. I wasn't sure what was true or manufactured by a little girl's creative imagination or a brain's self-defense mechanism that deleted memories and made others up. I knew my brain did what it needed to do to protect me.

By that point, I had been in therapy for years—unpacking the fuzzy bits, trying to make sense of various behaviors and beliefs I took on at different stages of my life. I was struggling to unearth the truth—my truth. At some point, I realized—with the help of my therapist—that it would be beneficial to share what I was remembering with my family in the hopes they could confirm some of what I was remembering and help me fill in some gaps.

But I was afraid that instead of filling the gaps, their memories would create more.

It took me more than a few months to get up the courage to set a plan in motion. I called Jack first. He was supportive and sweet and said yes right away. After some heart-thumping phone calls with Maddy, Cindy, and Ryan, they all reluctantly agreed to meet.

Dayna, my therapist, had wisely suggested a neutral location for such a sensitive conversation. Because I lived the farthest away, I set it up for right before Thanksgiving 1996, when we'd all be in Connecticut together at Cindy's for one of our annual family gatherings.

Dad had died about seven years prior, and Mom had been gone almost nine. Since then, it had been as if my siblings and I were scattered particles that had lost our nucleus. Since our parents' deaths, holidays became a powerful interatomic force that pulled us together at least once or twice a year. We willingly traveled from four different states despite it being crazy times in our lives with growing families and careers. Cindy and her husband, James, would often host.

As I had requested, the date and time for this "family meeting" was agreed upon. I rented an inexpensive room at a convenient highway motel. It offered basic rooms designed to meet the minimum needs of travelers en route to somewhere. Like most of the motel's temporary residents, I, too, hoped to leave that room to get to a better place. My destination was clarity, connection, honesty, and healing.

With hope in my heart and fear in my bones, I had done it. Summoned my siblings for "the talk." I yearned to know and to come to a better understanding of what happened in the junkyard. I wasn't sure what to expect, which was the point.

One moment, I felt so terrified I didn't know if I could speak, and the next, I was so elated at the prospect of finally giving voice to the questions and memories I was sorting through on my own. Was this selfish? Yes, I was doing this for myself, but I wondered if this bring up stuff my siblings had buried long ago and didn't want to look at. Would it help my siblings heal as well?

When I asked Cindy about coming, her soft and shaky voice had asked, "Why do you need to bring all this up now?" Cindy would never express anger or disagree publicly with anyone, so while it was out of character for her to question a request, I wasn't surprised. I was asking a lot of my sisters and brothers.

I was asking them to face stuff they had long buried.

We all had our own secrets, yet, I was opening them up to have to face them and possibly share them.

Shit.

I wanted so desperately to know, but I also didn't. I was so comfortable pretending. Why couldn't I just keep doing that? Pretending had worked well so far, hadn't it?

As time went on, I got in touch with the part of me deep inside that knew that this was something I had to do.

It was an essential part of my healing journey to share what I remembered and learn from other family members what had happened. There were many questions I had hoped I'd find answers. Did Mr. P do anything to anyone else? Did they know? Did they think Mom and Dad knew? Was I making all this up? When did it all start?

Rich was encouraging and supportive. He drove me to that meeting about six hours away from our home in Upstate New York. When we pulled up to drop me off at the motel carport entrance, I wasn't sure if I could open the car door to get out, let alone face all of them in that room. "You can do this," he said. "You'll feel so much better no matter what you learn."

I may have mumbled something like—yeah—and as the cold November air hit my face, I proceeded to propel myself out of the car and into the lobby.

I don't remember checking in. I just recall that moment when I was facing Maddy, Cindy, Jack, and Ryan, all of us awkwardly trying to appear comfortable as we sat on the two double beds in the simple hotel room. Just as I couldn't determine when and how the large and noisy in-room heating unit would come to life and reach a crescendo of spits and spurs indicating heat would soon arrive, I never could have imagined what I would soon learn.

Broken Silence–Part 2

I FELT IT.

All of their eyes were on me.

Remembering the cues my therapist had suggested, I took a breath, and knowing they were looking at me, eyes wide in anticipation, I closed mine for just a moment. I heard my therapist's words in my head, *"Take your time. You can do this."*

I relaxed despite the awkwardness of the silence punctuated by that damn heater making a racket. Then, I sensed something in the air beside the stale, slightly pine disinfectant scent.

What was it?

Then I felt deeper.

I was feeling all of our questions.

The anxiety.

The angst.

The heaviness of why the junkyard kids were all gathered, waiting uncomfortably for me to start bringing some of our darkest secrets into the light. To break the silence about things we had never talked about.

Opening my eyes, I looked up at us all—coats and hats shoved aside, lack of sleep, or long drives worn on our faces. Then I felt what I had unknowingly been waiting for. I felt fear—but surrounding that, a softness. I felt love.

A love that grew among all the junk and broken glass surrounding us. A love that brought us together in this room at that moment—despite how hard it was.

A love that was capable of anything.

Fueled by this, I took a sip of lukewarm tap water from the sterile wax paper cup I had filled from the bathroom sink.

Watching them watch me, I felt brave.

Clearing my throat, I started by thanking them for coming and reiterated what I had said on the phone to each of them. That I needed to do this to clarify some things I didn't remember clearly about Mr. P and what he did to me—what he may have done to them. I reassured them they didn't have to share anything they didn't want to.

There was silence, and then Jack came to my rescue and said, "Okay, let's get this started then." So that's what we did.

While I don't remember exactly what I said, I imagine I shared any number of fractured memories that were coming to me in therapy at that time.

Flashes of scenes as if I were seeing them on a movie screen.

His mostly unclothed body, looming over me while I was in my bed sleeping. Groggily awakened to the smell of grease and sweat and him trying to suppress grunts and moans as he watched me—and sometimes Maddy as we slept. He would look down at me—his face dark and in the shadow back-lit from the hallway light. He was in the shadows, where he belonged.

I recalled the odd crooked smile on his face as he touched himself. Watching me watch him. It makes my stomach turn to think of the pleasure this gave him. I didn't understand anything. I was not fully awake, and it felt like a bad dream. No, a nightmare—especially when I awoke the next morning. And to be honest, even now, more than fifty years later.

Other times, he made me touch *it*. Sometimes while we were watching a TV show with him in his room. I remember being excited to watch *Bewitched*, *Green Acres*, or *The Brady Bunch* on the little TV he had on his dresser right next to his twin bed. I'd get settled next to him on his bed as he adjusted the rabbit ears on the set to get the picture just right.

He always wore these short shorts he'd cut from a pair of jeans. They were short—but the leg openings were roomy enough for him to guide my hand to where he wanted it to be. He'd silently move my hand in the direction he wanted it to go. Me watching the screen intently so I could pretend my hand wasn't mine. It was someone else's. My little hand and arm muscles grew tired but afraid to stop until I knew from the cadence of his breath and the sudden jerk he'd make that he was finished. Then I could let go, wipe my hands on his bedspread, and watch until the show ended.

I know I didn't share this at the meeting, but I was beginning to recall specific painful memories of how when I was a little older, we'd go for drives and do more. Sometimes it hurt—but I think somehow he liked that. He used to tell me to "lick his lollipop," and he'd guide my mouth, sometimes not so gently, to where he wanted me to lick.

Afterward, we'd usually stop to get an ice cream cone on the way home.

At this point, I looked up to see my siblings in the hotel room.

All of our eyes were now averting each other. I had exposed something unthinkable. I had spoken the unspeakable. I had revealed the truth.

Each of us was there—but trying not to be there.

Suddenly our environment took center stage. Inspecting our hands— noticing the need for a manicure or dry skin. Staring down at the stains we could now see in the sculpted shag carpet that had god knows what else on it. Or gliding our fingers across the synthetic fabric of the ugly quilted bedspreads we were sitting on, making a slightly audible scratchy sound.

I looked up at Ryan. The eldest. His head bent, and he looked down at his hands. He said sadly, "I'm so sorry. So sorry I wasn't there." Ryan, for the most part, had been gone by then. He had left to go to the West Coast to go to college and find his future. He didn't know about any of this. I wonder if later—or reading these words I'm writing now—if he would feel guilty. I hope not. There really was nothing he could have done.

Tears filled Cindy's big, beautiful eyes as she told us she didn't know. Her head shaking in her hands, she softly mentioned that she had made a deal to have sex with Mr. P to protect us. She thought he had never touched us. "I'm so sorry," her faint voice said. "I never knew, Laurie. I thought he had left you all alone."

Jack was fidgety and silent. I am not sure if he planned to tell us, but he did eventually share how he was molested by Mr. P, too. He tried to hide the pain of his words, but I could see it was there.

I felt the air get thicker and heavier. We all did.

Years later, during many supportive phone conversations, Jack would share memories coming back to him, too. He said that Mr. P had come to him also in the night and believed that was the source of his chronic insomnia and night terrors that are happening decades later.

I couldn't imagine my little brother going to sleep—and having to wake up—in that room with that monster. Each night, not knowing if tonight would be a night he'd awaken to live what would become a nightmare that would cause severe insomnia, anxiety, and depression for the rest of his life.

I remember a photo of Jack with an aviator cap on as he slept. He must have been eight or nine. I wonder if he somehow imagined it would protect him. Too bad it didn't. Pretending may not be that powerful after all.

Maddy was twirling her long blonde hair around her fingers. She seemed to be trying to work something out in her head.

Eventually, she said, "I remember him doing those things while we watched TV too." Then she paused and started to cry. "I tried so hard to protect you, Laurie. I knew something was going on. I remember leaning against our closed bedroom door to keep him out." Then she held her head in her hands and said, "I don't remember him touching me."

I felt for Maddy. Years later, she confessed that she, too, was abused by Mr. P. I wish she didn't have to feel "special" the way I did. I wouldn't wish that on anyone.

After we'd all shared what we needed to say, we sat there feeling the enormity of what had been said. As the radiator became the dominant sound in the room, we started to get ready to leave.

I heard more truth than I could ever have imagined that day. It would take me years to unravel it.

That meeting began something.

Jack thanked me years later, telling me that was the start of his healing journey. Maddy, too, has been doing her own healing work.

It was in that room on that day the five of us strengthened a bond that, to this day, keeps us a family. We were then—as we are now—there for each other no matter what. That day, each of us took away what we needed. It may have been validation, knowledge, or permission to deal with what was said however we needed to.

For Cindy—maybe it was to keep those secrets safe inside so she could be the amazingly warm and loving woman, friend, wife, mother, sister, and grandmother she is today. She is so selfless—willing to do anything she can for anyone. Just like she tried to sacrifice herself for us so many years ago. That is so like her.

While Ryan couldn't be there for us then, I know he would be there any time we needed anything now. He is the one who will hop in the car—no questions asked—anytime, day or night, to drive eight or ten hours to be with you.

Maddy, a successful professional, gives so much to her family and friends and offers her support to others who need it. She is strong in spirit and is always ready to fight for what she believes is right.

Jack and I got closer because of what we shared in that room. It's a connection that has only strengthened as we support each other on our healing journeys today. I have forgiven Mr. P for what he did to me. I will never forgive him for what he did to Jack.

That Thanksgiving was the first time in my life I believe I felt gratitude. I felt truly grateful. Thankful for the love, compassion, and even for the anger of it all. Indebted to my family for showing up for me that year like they did. Grateful the silence was broken.

Eagle Scout

BLIND DATES WORK. MY HUSBAND AND I ARE PROOF. OVER THIRTY-EIGHT YEARS ago, while working at IBM in the communications department, a friend kept pestering me to meet a friend of his in "production control." Perhaps I was supposed to be impressed, but it didn't sound too promising. "I really think you two would hit it off," Mark insisted. "I really do."

Mark kept asking. We both kept saying no.

The phone rang one morning while I was sitting at my desk in my cubicle. I picked up. "Hey, how about we go to Andy and Steve's today for chili? Meet there at noon?" Mark wasted no time asking. "Okay, I'll see you there," I replied, and before I could even confirm, he hung up. It was so not like him not to want to chat.

I arrived at Andy and Steve's with a girlfriend at the appointed time, mouth already watering for the only thing on the menu—fantastic chili. Andy and Steve started the restaurant after too many friends and family people kept asking for Steve's chili recipe. The menu was simple: chili and cheese, chili and onions, and chili and onions and cheese. Oh, and they had homemade bread on the side that was soft and warm from the oven. Yum! The place was a hit. Open only Monday through Friday, it was packed with IBMers each lunch hour. They even had specials where if you showed your IBM badge, you'd get a brownie or cookie for dessert.

As soon as I descended the steps into the restaurant's basement, my eyes adjusted to the light, and I scanned the crowd for Mark. I saw his smiling face, along with a few of Mark's friends, and next to him sat a sandy-haired, thin guy nervously looking toward me as well. You guessed it—this turned out to be Rich. I grinned back at Mark, silently sending him pissed-off vibes, but I sat down and said, "You must be Rich. Nice to meet you."

Mark replied, beaming, "Yes, Laurie meet Rich. Rich meet Laurie. Finally, I've got the two of you to meet!" He was beside himself with accomplishment. Lunch, as always, was excellent. The group made chatting easy for Rich and me without feeling uncomfortable. Mark beamed when he noticed us exchanging phone numbers.

A week or so later, Rich asked me if I'd like to go sailing with him on the Hudson River. I hadn't sailed since high school and, to be honest, was impressed he owned a sailboat. I figured why not, so I said yes, and we set a date for an upcoming Saturday, weather permitting.

Once aboard the 24-foot *O'Day*, he told me he was a Sea Scout leader, a division of scouting called Explorer Scouting that taught girls and boys to sail. This and several other boats were part of the Sea Scout fleet. As we sailed, Rich relaxed and told me how much he loved sailing and sharing his passion and knowledge with kids. I could see he really enjoyed being a scout leader. He was a natural leader and sailor. He told me he learned to sail with his dad on a small lake in the Finger Lakes where he grew up. His awkwardness began to ease as his face became animated, sharing stories of racing with his dad and a few sailing mishaps and trips he took the sea scouts on, including sailing down the Hudson and around Manhattan, navigating New York Harbor and the difficult and dangerous tides.

Rich was at ease on the water, and I was at ease with him. The time flew. Before we knew it, we were back docking at the marina. We both didn't want the date to end. We continued to chat as Rich walked me to my car when he asked if I happened to be free that night to go with a few other friends from IBM to the Bear Mountain Inn. I quickly said yes.

That was our first date, and almost forty years later, we still talk about that entire day—especially that night because we won a dance contest we hadn't even known we had entered. We danced and talked so much that we didn't notice they had announced a dance contest. We just kept dancing and never noticed that the number of couples dancing alongside us had dwindled until we were the only two left, and they handed us the first prize!

I don't know which had more bubbles, my insides or the bottle of champagne we won. Rich was the ultimate gentleman. Not used to that, I worried he didn't like me because as much as I wished it, he didn't even try to hold my hand—let alone kiss me—as we sat right next to one another in the backseat of the car on the long ride home.

As I lay in bed that night, I couldn't sleep. I kept running through the entire day and evening. *Had I said or done something wrong? Would he call me again?*

Rich did call, and he was the ultimate gentleman not just that night but for several more. It gave us time to get to know each other. I realized that two words describe what attracted me and keep me loving Rich.

Eagle. Scout.

Rich was quite proud that he was among the few who had reached the coveted rank of Eagle Scout during high school. Then and today, he is a man who embodies trustworthiness, honesty, caring, always being prepared, servant leadership, and a daily commitment to lifelong learning.

My friends would tell me, "He isn't your type," and at first, I wasn't sure he was. He seemed so nerdy. Just after our first date, he mentioned he was so excited that he had special ordered a new car from the dealer and couldn't wait until it arrived. He kept talking about it for weeks. He had special ordered the car's color, including requesting specific upholstery.

I don't know what type of car I expected, but I didn't expect him to pull up proudly in a gold hatchback Dodge Daytona. It was shiny gold. I mean, shiny like gold lamé. Inside was a black and gray interior. As soon as I hopped in, he couldn't contain himself. He was so excited I couldn't help but think it was cute. "How do you like it?" he quizzed me before I even closed the passenger-side door. "Wow," I said. "This is nice." I looked around at the new interior and asked, "Why did you want a gold car?"

"It was my high school color," he proudly replied as if it made perfect sense for a grown man in his twenties to purchase his first brand new car to commemorate his high school alma mater. It was a very nice car, especially compared to the junkers I was used to, but I never got over that he actually special ordered that color. We turned heads for years in that car. I don't think I've ever seen another car that color.

BR (before Rich), I thought I knew my type. I had constantly compared other guys, including Rich, to my old boyfriend, who I wanted to believe was my type—sophisticated, polished, mysterious, and fashionable.

While Bill was my first love, Rich is my true love. Rich was my anti-Bill. He was (and is still) a bit of a sweet, innocent nerd. A few months after we started dating, I knew something was there because I wasn't "pretending" with Rich.

At one point, I had a terrible flu and missed several work days. I was a real mess. Rich called to ask how I was. Without thinking, I told him he could stop over. I can't believe I answered the door smelling of vomit, hair dirty and matted, wearing my oldest ripped but comfy PJs, and looking like death. Rich came right in bearing chicken noodle soup from the deli. He straightened up the tissues strewn about the living room, emptied and cleaned my "throw-up bucket," and stayed with me for hours, fetching me ginger ale and even tidying up my kitchen.

That was a turning point for me. I began to recognize that I was more myself with him. I wasn't planning what to say ahead of time. I didn't need to make sure everything looked perfect. I wasn't controlling the version of Laurie I wanted him to see. Slowly, my guard dissolved, and I could open up not just to him, but to myself. The more I was with Rich, the more I began to unearth who I was. He helped me discover what I really liked and wanted. Rich was genuinely interested in who

I was—not just what I could do for him. He really listened to me. I had never felt seen like that before. It slowly opened up something in me. Something that sometimes I shut back down, but I knew there was something underneath worth uncovering.

Despite this deep connection, there was one thing that took a bit for me to get over as we got to know one another. It was Rich's wardrobe.

He dressed like an Eagle Scout. No, he didn't wear the scouting uniform (although he proudly showed it to me once). Rich wore his clothing as if it were a uniform.

I had a large picture window right next to my front door, which gave me a clear view of whoever was approaching as they ascended the stairs to my apartment. After a month of dating, I could predict, with almost 100 percent accuracy, what his entire ensemble would be just by seeing what he was wearing on his top half as he climbed the stairs. It became a game I'd play. As I saw his head bopping up the stairs and his shirt or sweater were slowly revealed, in my mind, I'd select the pants he'd be wearing down to his footwear. I was right more times than wrong.

Later, I learned he wore his clothes in matching pairs based on the gift box they had come in from his mother. He told me with shaky confidence, "My mom is good at picking out my clothes. So I figured if my mom had picked out this shirt and these pants, they must match. It made it easy for me. . . and. . . ahh. . . I just wanted to be sure I looked okay." He quickly asked, "I do look okay, don't I?" His cute factor went up as he innocently explained his logic.

When I heard that, I had a business brainstorm. I'd design a safe way for men like Rich to have a fashionable and varied wardrobe without risking a fashion faux pas. It would be a grown-up Garanimals label for a menswear line that offered a simple label system to make it easy for men to be confident that their outfit choice matched by checking the tag inside the garment. Along with the care instructions, the label would display simple symbols. Simply matching the same symbol found on the label inside a particular shirt, sweater, or pants –meant you could wear them together. For example, if you saw a purple triangle on each item, it was a match! I was proud of this idea, thinking it would take the guesswork out of clothing choices for men like Rich and give him more variety in his wardrobe choices.

I never did follow through with this brilliant idea; however, even to this day, whenever I see some poor soul sporting a mismatched or outdated outfit, I still feel its merit. Eventually, Rich figured out his own taste with a bit of help from me. Years later, his style was honed in by guidance from our three daughters, as they would veto or approve his clothing choices throughout the years.

I love his genuine nerdiness when it comes out. He is my Eagle Scout, and I love him for it. He is and was the perfect partner to support me during the thirty years of healing myself so I could find my way to myself.

Dirty Diamonds

OFTEN IN MADDY'S AND MY SHADOW, JACK WAS ALWAYS THERE. READY FOR anything. Typical of the youngest, Jack didn't want to miss anything. He wanted to tag along and be a part of whatever was happening. I understood that feeling of longing. Wanting to fit in. I imagine we all did. Yet, this may have been part of what drew Jack and me together. Unfortunately, we shared another deeper connection, thanks to Mr. P and his perverted ways.

After a false start in college, Jack lied to Mom and Dad for a few semesters, pretending to be enrolled in classes but taking his tuition to fund a punk rock band. Jack was a talented musician. I remember one of the first times I saw him perform. It was with his band Beached Black in the eighties at some hole-in-the-wall bar in New London, Connecticut. There was my little brother, wild hair flying and covering his sweaty face as he jerked and moved behind a mismatched and patched-up drum kit, banging the shit out of the drums.

Don't get me wrong, it sounded great. But I remember seeing him giving his all to those drums. There he was, this whirlwind of energy, arms flailing as he pounded on the drums as if his life depended on it. He crashed the cymbals with reckless abandon, beads of sweat flying off him into the air. He was lost in the music.

Later that night, I wondered where all this aggression was coming from. It surprised me. Little Jack, who was so quick to please all of us in his childhood, was perhaps finding his way. No longer doing whatever was asked of him. Jack, who was so comfortable in the shadows, was now seeking the spotlight. Years later, I would understand.

As Jack has worked to heal his wounds from our childhood, drumming has continued to play a role. He left the entertainment world after he faced his demons of depression, anxiety, and addiction. Eventually, he became an addiction counselor, leading healing drum circles with his patients. Jack may not have known it when he started drumming with our uncle in the marching drum corps or when he began to perform in bands, but drumming helps release and process powerful emotions, many stemming from trauma, abuse, grief, sadness, and pain.

When Jack and I began our healing journeys as adults, we were there for each other every step of the way. We understood. We called each other often. In one conversation, I shared my fears about writing and eventually publishing my story. It wasn't long before we were both crying, recognizing how our stories connect us deeply. "Laurie," Jack's shaky, emotional voice said between tearful pauses, "I am so grateful for you."

"You know," he continued, chuckling a bit, "our connection is one of the diamonds from the dirt."

True Reflection

I WAS ALWAYS TOLD THERE WAS A SIGNIFICANT DIFFERENCE BETWEEN WANTING and needing. They were independent of each other.

When I held up a book, toy, or piece of candy at the store, begging Mom to buy it, her reply would always be, "Not today. We don't need that." When I really wanted to tell someone what was happening to me as a child, I convinced myself that no, I didn't need to do that. That what I needed was to pretend all was okay, and maybe it would be.

I learned that what we want is often so different from what we need.

It took me years to unlearn this and to recognize I disagreed whole-heartedly. I spent decades desperately wanting what I needed without knowing it was a primordial desire, a fundamental core human need.

I rarely got what I wanted and needed, but what I needed and wanted were the same thing.

I craved real connection, love, and acceptance. Don't we all? Isn't that why children jump up and down, screaming for our attention? You can't visit a playground or public pool in the heat of the summer without hearing a chorus of kids screaming, "Mom, look at me? Did you see that I just did a dive all by myself?" "Mom. Mom. MOM. LOOK AT ME!!!"

Look at me.

See me.

Love me.

I wanted the right people to look and see me and to approve of what they saw. I needed external validation to believe from my core that I was okay. I didn't need to be the best. Or perfect. I just wanted to be okay. It would have been enough to know I was enough.

Was it that I craved to see the me they saw? Perhaps I convinced myself that if I could see clearly the reflection of the me that they saw, the me I was pretending to be, then maybe that could be true. That I was a good person. Someone who shined despite the fact I felt dull and dirty on the inside.

I spent years seeking myself by scrutinizing the reflection of what others saw in me. If the me I saw reflected back was pleasing, okay, and acceptable, then I must be okay!

I franticly sought this validation from teachers at school by achieving excellent grades, participating, and contributing. From the audiences at musical concerts, plays, and performances. From my high school boyfriend Cody and his family because they were normal, and if I fit in and saw myself as they saw me and I fit there, I must be normal too. I became skillful at playing along as my amoeba-like self-morphed into whoever the situation necessitated I become. This was the only way I knew how to have a chance at being loved, seen, and accepted.

I knew there were things about me, our life in the junkyard, I had to hide. Fear prevented me from truly being me. Shame blocked the shiny me—the me that I now know as brilliant and bright—the me that has always been worthy of love.

During my decades-long healing journey in my thirties and forties, "mirror" work helped me to see the real me. A therapist had me hold a mirror up to my face and really, really look at the face staring back at me. As I healed, the face I saw changed—just as I had shown others different versions of who I thought I was for years. This time, my reflection helped me heal.

I saw the tiny, scared little girl, afraid and alone. And I comforted her. I held her. Telling her it wasn't her fault.

I saw the pretender with a fake smile others took as real. I forgave her. I told her she had been skillful at doing that all those years and didn't need to do that anymore.

I saw the strong one whose resilience shone in her determined face. I thanked her and let her know she could relax now. She could rest.

I saw the broken woman whose wounds covered her desire and sexuality with shame. I let her feel safe. I let her explore. I gave her permission to want and need. I taught her it was safe to let go. I helped her be vulnerable.

Eventually, I recognized the woman reflected in the mirror as me. A woman with emotional scars of wounds she had worked so hard to heal. I told her that she was more than okay. That, while she may feel damaged, she was whole and amazing.

My reflection taught me it's okay to want and need and, better yet, to ask for what I want and need. And this woman gracefully asks—and lovingly receives.

Grateful Heart

I SHUT THE THICK, SOLID FRONT DOOR BEHIND ME, PAUSING TO BE SURE I HAD everything. Carefully, I make my way down the hundred-year-old steps, noticing the string of lights we had hung and remnants of the welcome party we had last night, with forty or fifty of our family and friends gathered from all over the country to be with us for today's celebration.

Gingerly, I walked along our curvy crushed rock driveway in my sensible but dressy shoes, gathering a bit of the length of my long mother-of-the-bride dress in my hand so it didn't drag on the ground.

Hearing a breeze gently moving the tree leaves above, I looked up and noticed the sun trying to peek out of the clouds. The trees were my witness, standing tall and surrounding our home as they always have. I thought to myself, *what stories could they tell about our life here for the past thirty years?* I felt another seed of gratitude for this home, this life Rich and I had created, as I stepped away from it, crossing the street toward Sonnenberg Garden and Mansion State Park.

I turned and looked back at our Victorian home, set back in the wooded lot, standing tall and graceful among the ancient trees surrounding it, the trees that, a hundred years ago, were planted by the gardener of the Sonnenberg estate. The history of our home swirls with my own history, grounding me with every step I took.

I stepped onto the garden grounds via the back entrance, as I had done hundreds of times. I turned right, following the flagstone path that took me under the canopy of the trees to the rock garden, where the wedding ceremony would take place in just a few hours. I noticed bits of sun continuing to shine through the lace of leaves above me. Feeling a light breeze on my shoulders, I was grateful no rain clouds were in sight. I felt calm.

I closed my eyes and took a breath. Happy I could take this short walk and have this moment to myself.

My eldest daughter Liz was soon to become a wife under these very trees and in this garden where I paced when I was nine months pregnant with her. Where months later I would stroll with her to get her to settle down and sleep. Where years later, I would help her unpack elaborate teddy bear picnics with her sisters. Where even later, she would pose for high-school prom pictures.

How life can come full circle.

Another breath, and I felt warmth radiate from my heart throughout my body. I felt so very grateful for my life and all the moments that had brought me to this day- moments that have caused me pain as well as joy.

I stand here as a mother, wife, and woman, having built an amazing life where I was seen and loved for who I am—faults and all. As I walked toward the bridal suite where Liz was getting ready, I smiled, knowing that my precious and close family will surround me and friends will celebrate love and family in just a few hours.

Another spec of junkyard dirt was shaken off as the sun emerged from behind a cloud. I walked toward the mansion where Liz and her bridal party were waiting and noticed the bright ball of sunshine shining down on me. I smiled as I walk into the room.

"Everything okay, Mom?" Liz asks.

"Yes," I say, my heart full of love, light, and gratitude. "Yes, it is."

Acknowledgments

WRITING THIS BOOK HAS BEEN A LONG TIME COMING. WHEN I WALKED INTO RENEE Schuls-Jacobson's writing class at Writers and Books in Rochester, New York, six years ago, I never knew I'd write enough stories to fill these pages. Sharing my story has been a healing journey for me.

Many thanks to the teachers and fellow writers who have read my pages, offering feedback and encouraging me to keep writing and become a published author. (Even now, as I write that, I can't believe it!)

Sue Collier of Author Allies guided me in the publishing process, gracefully kept me on track, and expertly edited the final manuscript. Suzi van der Sterre, of van der Sterre Design, for the cover design and the beautiful book layout.

Special thanks to many of my fellow writers: Bridget Dee, Kathy Kurtz, my Badass Sisters, Ellen Newman, Jackie Alcalde Marr, Terri Tomoff, and many other writers I met in Writer's In Community (you all know who you are), Canandaigua Writers Group, Haven Nest, and so many teachers, including Laura Munson, Lisa Cooper Ellison, and Jane Friedman for sharing your insights and encouragement about the gnarly and rewarding writing process.

I appreciate the care and time it took for my beta readers to offer valuable feedback, primarily as I worked on the structure of this book. I struggled to share my fuzzy memories authentically while honoring how fragmented and disjointed they were for me. Your insights helped me be true to myself and make this book a better read.

I couldn't have done this without my full manuscript beta readers: Stephanie Kemp, Pebble Kranz, Kate Kenney, T-Ann Pierce, Sandra Holy, and the amazing Susan Walter, who never failed to answer my many SOS calls, texts, and emails, and was with me every step of the way. You, my dear Susan, are among the many diamonds I have mined in this process.

I am blessed to have so many dear friends—too many to list here—but I hope you know who you are as you have been my greatest cheerleaders when I needed it on our walks, gatherings, and during phone and Zoom calls.

I've heard it said that family is like the many branches on a tree—they may grow in different directions, but our roots remain the same.

To my siblings, I am so very thankful that the roots of our tree are strong and run deep. I appreciate your willingness to answer my countless emails, texts, and calls as I struggled to recall and refine the fuzzy details of our life in the junkyard.

I recognize how difficult it may have been for you to relive memories of your life, especially those you did not wish to revisit. Your openness and support as I worked through the details of these stories, especially when some of my recollections differed from yours, have given me yet another unexpected gift in this process. I am deeply grateful for all those moments—the difficult and the joyous—and how fortunate we are to have a family like ours. Mom and Dad would be proud of us.

Thanks to the sisters-in-law! Pam Coyle, I don't know who is luckier—my brother or me—to have you in our life. Your encouragement, wise edits, and counsel helped me become a better writer. I bow to your creative mind as I have you to thank for the title of this book! Also, I can't thank you enough for introducing me to *your* sister-in-law, Ruby Privateer, editor extraordinaire, whose developmental edits and questions helped me polish my manuscript to become the one you are holding in your hands.

My heart aches as I feel the magnitude of my gratitude for my husband, Rich. This book would not be possible without him by my side every step of the way. You held me during all the years of digging deep into the muck and dirt and have walked along my side as I found my way to wholeness.

You helped me heal, write, own, and share my story. You have worked with me to open me up to being able to love you in ways I never thought possible. As you so often say to me, "I love you so much it hurts."

To my daughters, Liz, Beck, and Hannah, thank you for being you and showing me how to let go and be. Parenting you allowed me to look deep into my childhood and help me connect with and heal "little Laurie." You have given my life meaning, and I love you very much.

And a book would not be a book without its readers. So thanks to you, my dear readers, here and on my Substack blog, More Than Words. You honor me by reading my words and inspire me to continue to mine the gifts in my life and let my light shine for all to see. If you would like to get in touch with me reach out via www.laurieriedman.com.

Afterword

Sharing stories about the events and people in my life that shaped me has been transformational.

It hasn't been easy, but writing these stories invited me to look honestly at my life and appreciate all it has given me, including how grief and pain co-existed with childlike wonder, fun, and love. Recalling these memories and life events has shown me, so very clearly, how the creative power of pretend sparked foundational resiliency—and saved me.

I have come to a peaceful place of acceptance of my past, but when writing about people you love, you risk hurting them with your truth. Because of the stories' personal and, at times, painful nature, I changed most names. My goal is not to hurt but to be heard, as being heard is an essential human need. My intention has been to gracefully and carefully share my story without compromising or hurting those who were and are part of it.

Memory is curious and confusing, especially for someone with childhood trauma.

As I began writing and sharing my memories with my family, I discovered that the protective power of my brain altered or erased parts of my memory. Some of the gaps and discrepancies between details my siblings and I remember made me feel like I lived in a different family.

For example, in One Dollar and Seventy-Nine Cents, I vividly recall the feeling of being special as my grandmother drove me in her fancy car. Yet, when I called my older brother Ryan to confirm the car's make and model, he said she never drove. That she was afraid to. We decided that perhaps Mom was driving, and because I wanted so badly to have time alone with Grandma and to feel special, my brain altered the facts. The power of pretend did indeed save me as it rewrote what happened sometimes.

This may happen to you, too.

I wrote the stories here as I remembered them. I did reach out to many friends and family to recall details, jog memories, and fill in the gaps. I tried my best to research and include accurate information by traveling to Higganum several times to visit locations I describe in my stories—including our simple cedar-shingled home, now the office for a junkyard still in operation there.

Writing my story helped me make sense of my life and own my truth. I have shared my truth in the hopes that my words and stories can encourage my readers to discover their own.

Here's to owning and sharing our stories, my friends. The truth is that while it is difficult to do—it will bring us closer. Closer to ourselves—our authentic selves—and closer to each other.

I also hope these stories inspire you to savor the gifts of your own life, mine the gold there, and heal the wounds of your past. I am a stronger woman living a fulfilling and happy life. It is possible to move forward when bad things happen to you.

Thank you for hearing my story.

About the Author

Laurie Riedman is a personal and relationship coach, writer, and story-teller. After thirty-five years running her own PR and marketing firm, she transitioned her consulting to coaching, founding b.u. coaching to support those—like her—who seek to embrace their truths and be their best selves in all aspects of their personal and professional lives.

Writing and publishing essays on her blog More Than Words and publishing her memoir *Diamonds in the Dirt: Stories From a Junkyard Girl* are part of her healing journey. She has also published essays in *Bluff and Vine*. Her writing is included in two anthologies—one she co-edited with Susan Walter titled *Badass Sisterhood* and the forthcoming *Soul Shine*. For more information on her writing life visit www.laurieriedman.com

Laurie lives, writes, and coaches from her home along Canandaigua Lake in the Finger Lakes of New York. Married to her life partner Rich for over thirty-eight years, they have founded three successful companies and raised three amazing daughters: Elizabeth, Beck, and Hannah.